Heinz A. Richter

German-Greek Relations 1940-1960

And the Merten Affair

Peleus

Studien zur Geschichte Griechenlands und Zyperns

Herausgegeben von Heinz A. Richter

Band 90

HARRASSOWITZ VERLAG WIESBADEN
IN KOMMISSION

VORMALS VERLAG FRANZ PHILIPP RUTZEN
WWW.RUTZEN-VERLAG.DE

Heinz A. Richter

German-Greek Relations 1940-1960

and the Merten Affair

2019

HARRASSOWITZ VERLAG • WIESBADEN
IN KOMMISSION

PELEUS
Studien zur Geschichte Griechenlands und Zyperns
Herausgegeben von Heinz A. Richter
Band 90

Umschlagvignetten:
Umschlagbild: Merten vor Gericht
Gegenüber Titelblatt: Innenbild einer Schale des Peithinosmalers, Berlin, Pergamonmuseum (CVA Berlin 2, Taf. 61).

Bibliografische Information der Deutschen Nationalbibliothek
Die Deutsche Nationalbibliothek verzeichnet diese Publikation in der Deutschen Nationalbibliografie; detaillierte bibliografische Daten sind im Internet über http://dnb.d-nb.de abrufbar.

Bibliographic information published by the Deutsche Nationalbibliothek
The Deutsche Nationalbibliothek lists this publication in the Deutsche Nationalbibliografie; detailed bibliographic data are available in the internet at http://dnb.d-nb.de

Printed in Germany on fade resistant and archival quality paper (PH 7 neutral).
Gesamtherstellung: Beltz Bad Langensalza GmbH, Bad Langensalza

www.harrassowitz-verlag.de

ISBN 978-3-447-11177-5
ISSN 1868-1476

I dedicate this study to my former publisher and close friend

Franz Rutzen

and to his late wife Eva

CONTENT

INTRODUCTION

Almost the whole historical literature, no matter whether in English, Greek or German considers Max Merten as a war criminal. According to these studies he was responsible for the deportation of the Jews of Salonika to Auschwitz, for the shooting of hundreds of hostages and for the stealing of Jewish property. Most astonishing, however, is the fact that the highly respectable newspaper, *Die Frankfurter Allgemeine Sonntagszeitung*, published an article in the same tenor in April 2015.[1] A scholarly study published in 2018 stated that Merten had played a hypocritical role and this had allegedly been proven by actual research.[2] The few German studies which reached different conclusions were not taken note of. In March 1959 Merten was sentenced to 25 years of prison in Athens. This was really astonishing because in 1945 the Greek commissioner in Germany, General Ypsilantis, had stated, when the Americans offered to turn Merten over to Greece, that Merten had behaved blamelessly in Salonika and should be released instead. Even more astonishing, however, was the fact that eight months later he was released from prison and sent to Germany. If he really was a war criminal, how could he be discharged from prison so quickly? Or is it possible that the court in Athens committed a judicial error? If this were true, why did so many historians come to the conclusion that Merten was a war criminal?

In order to answer these question several fields of events outside and the developments insie occupied Greece must be analysed and described. The first fact is the question for the structure of occupation regime and the function of a *Kriegsverwaltungsrat*? This means, its powers and competences must be analysed. It is a fact that Merten signed the orders which has been prepared and led to the deportation of the Jews of Salonika, but did he sign these orders of his own authority or on orders by somebody else? As the answer to this question plays a decisive role in the deportation of the Jews it must be analysed thoroughly.

Did the authority of a *Kriegsverwaltungsrat* include the authorization to order the shooting of hostages? Could such a civil servant confiscate properties and steal them? Did Merten's alleged treasures really exist? Why was Merten

1 Reiner Burger, "Kriegsverbrechen: Die Märchen des Max Merten" *Frankfurter Allgemeine Sonntagszeitung* (19. 4. 2015).

2 Heike Christina Mätzing, *Georg Eckert 1912-1974. Von Anpassung, Widerstand und Völkerverständigung* (Bonn: Dietz, 2018), p. 253.

ordered to leave Greece in March 1944 and was moved north to Zagreb in Croatia?

Because later developments were closely linked with the question of reparations a close look must be taken at this topic. This requires the analysis of Greece's financial policy since 1832 when the new Greek state came into being. Since then the Greek budget always had a gap which was closed by the protecting powers. After WWII Greece like all other Western European countries received dismantled industrial goods from Germany which in the case of Greece never arrived there. The 1952 London debt agreement closed the door to further reparations. Therefore, the Greek Government began to search for other ways. Was the arresting of Merten in Athens somehow connected to the reparation question?

If Merten really was a war criminal, why was he set free after a few days after his return to Germany? Why was he not jailed as other war criminals were?

When Merten returned to Germany a new quarrel began with Adenauer's right hand, Hans Globke, who had played a major role in the persecution of the Jews. This makes it necessary to take a closer look at Globke's past during the Third Reich and to raise some new questions. Why did Globke not help Merten during his trial in Athens and why did he now indict Merten? It is known that Merten tried to attack Karamanlis and Makris and the wife of the latter. Was this a counterattack and an effort to seek revenge? In 1971 Merten died rather young at the age of 60. But this date did not end the story because in 1999 an intensive diving search began looking for Merten's hidden treasures. The analysis of this adventurous story shows that the Merten story has not reached its end.

At the end of this study I hope that I will be able to provide the reader with an answer to the question whether Merten was a war criminal or not and if he was guilty at all. However, it is not my intention to vidicate Merten but I am of the opinion that it is time that the historical truth comes to light.

As in all other English editions of my books I needed a final control by a native speaker. In this case it was my old friend Rodney Freeborg Ph. D. living in the US. I want to thank him most cordially for his readiness to correct the text.

Equally I want to thank my old friend Helmut Gernert for his diligent final correction.

MERTEN IN THE EARLY WAR YEARS

Merten's Early Carreer

Max Merten was born on 8 September 1911 in Berlin-Lichterfelde as son of Max Merten, deputy director of the department of town development (*Stadtkontor*) of Berlin, and of his wife, Rosa, née Ries. He was baptised Max by a protestant pastor.[1]

From 1918 to 1921 he attended primary school and a secondary school until 1930. He finished as the best of his class (primus omnium) with the *Abitur* (university-entrance diploma). The following three years he studied law at the University of Berlin. On 29 June 1933 he passed the first State Examination (*Staatsexamen*) with a good result. On 5 August he was promoted trainee solicitor (*Rechtsreferendar*) and on 9 August he was inaugurated. On 28 August 1934 the binding obligation of loyalty to the Führer followed. A little later he received his PhD with the qualification "rite". On 25 September 1936 he passed the second state examination with the qualification "good" and then he was appointed graduate civil servant (*Assessor*). Though Merten had studied during he final years of the Weimar Republic his exams took place in the beginning of the Third Reich and time of the enforced political conformity (*Gleichschaltung*).

After a month's interlude in a German wood company in November 1936, on 1 January 1937 he was accepted as a probationary civil servant of the judiciary of the province Berlin-Brandenburg. On 1 January 1938 he became assistant judge (Gerichtsassessor). The following six months he worked as an applicant for the office of a judge and prosecutor at the higher regional court of Nuremberg. In July 1938 he was transferred to the Ministry of Justice of the Reich in Berlin as an assistant and from then on he was an extraordinary civil servant. On 2 June 1939 he was promoted a regular civil servant with the rank of a full judge (*Landgerichtsrat*) in Berlin. From then on he worked as a specialist of law enforcement.

On 1 September 1939 WWII broke out. On 17 February 1940 Merten was exempted from military service by the military authorities for three months and on 4 April 1940 this was prolongated until further notice. From then on he tried to have this decision extended forever. The reason, why he was exemp-

---

1 The narrative follows: Wolfgang Breyer, "Dr. Max Merten - ein Militärbeamter der deutschen Wehrmacht im Spannungsfeld zwischen Legenden und Wahrheit" Diss. (Mannheim, 2002), p. 5f. Wolfgang Bryer was my oldest student. He received his doctoral degree at the age of 78.

ted from active service in the army was his grading as unfit for military service, due to an old sports injury of his left leg. He was considered as employable only in Germany.

On 18 November he married Erzsebet Sziklay, the daughter of a Hungarian diplomat. As the Hungarians did not belong to the Aryan race, Merten had to inform his superiors about his bride and ask for permission to marry her. After some to and fro Merten received the permission and got married. One day later, however, undersecretary of state, Roland Freisler, the future president of the notorious People's Court, ordered him to his office. For one hour Freisler spoke about the meaning of the Nuremberg racial laws and told Merten that the Hungarians were Gypsies. Then he gave Merten to understand that his marriage meant the end of his career with the ministry.[1] Merten's marriage with a non-Aryan woman can be interpreted that he was not convinced of the Nazi ideology.

Merten understood that he would loose his job and might encounter difficulties and applied to the Wehrmacht to become *Kriegsverwaltungsrat*. However, on 25 January 1942 he was drafted into active service as a gunner at an anti-aircraft unit in Stettin. But his service in this unit was cut short because already a few weeks later he was transferred to an air force centre in Berlin-Dahlem where he worked as a bureaucrat. On 27 July 1942 he received the order to go to Marburg where he would be promoted. On 28 June 1942 he was promoted war administrative officer (*Kriegsverwaltungsrat*). His place of employment would be the Greek island of Mytilini (Lesvos), from where the Reich imported 18,000 tons of olive oil annually. Merten's next stop was Vienna where he received his gear and his marching orders.

On the train he met his future superior, the *Kriegsverwaltungsoberrat* Dr. Parisius who was also travelling to Thessaloniki. When Parisius heard that Merten was heading for Mytilini he suggested that Merten should remain in Thessaloniki instead and replace *Kriegsverwaltungsrat* Dr. Karl Marbach who had become involved in a black market scandal which had created a lot of anger.[2] If Marbach remained in Salonika he would have to face a military court. Parisius wanted to replace him and asked Merten whether he would be ready to stay in Salonika. Merten agreed and Parisius requested him officially.[3] Thus on 10 August 1942 Merten was transferred to the army command Saloniki-Ägäis in Thessaloniki. On 1 October he took over the department of admini-

---

1 Claus Menzel, "Wenn Eichmann auspackt" *Hamburger Echo* (12. September 1960), p. 5
2 He had stolen Greek butter and schnapps. *Schleswig-Holsteinisches Landesarchiv*, Abt. 605, Nr. 3470.
3 *Ibidem* (12. September 1960), p. 5

stration and economy on the staff the of this command as a nominal captain, i.e. he wore a captain's uniform, but he remained a civilian in the service of the Wehrmacht.

After the war Merten denied that he had ever been a member of the NSDAP (Nazi-party). He knew that a membership would have negative consequences and he tried to avoid these. However, it is proven that he joined the party on 1 May 1937. He had the party number of the NSDAP 4,363,753.[1] But membership in the Nazi-Party did not necessarily mean that Merten was a Nazi by conviction. An example from my own personally experience may explain this.

My father was a teacher and a good Christian. In March 1933 a rumour circulated through all schools that all teachers who were not members of the NSDAP would be dismissed. Therefore, my father like most of his colleagues entered the party but he never became a Nazi by conviction. When the Jewish children were removed from all classes and put together in a separate one-room school, only my father was ready to teach them. He considered this his Christian duty. When the children were transported to the extermination camps the Nazis took their revenge: My father was transferred for disciplinary reasons to a school in a small village far in the country side. After the war he was banned from his profession for several years because he had been a party member.

Merten was also a member of the NSDAP. He entered the party fur similar motives as my father did. He knew that the doors to the civil service were closed to non-party members. However his later behaviour in Greece proved that he was not a Nazi by conviction as will be seen later in this study.

The German Attack in April 1941[2]

In order to understand later developments it appears reasonable that we first take a look at the events before and during the war which led to the occupation of Greece.

Greece was not part of Hitler's expansionist aims. When his first wars against Poland Denmark-Norway, Belgium-Netherlands and France were successful, Mussolini became jealous, put aside reason and on 10 June 1940 he joined Germany in the attack on France. His troops, however, failed miserably. The same happened during the Italian attack from Libya to Egypt and in East Africa a defeat was on the horizon. The Italian flyers which took part in

---

1 Breyer, *op. cit.*, p. 10f.

2 The narrative follows: Heinz A. Richter, *Griechenland im Zweiten Weltkrieg August 1939 - Juni 1941* [2](Ruhpolding: Rutzen, 2011) *passim*.

the battle of Britain failed, as did the Italian submarines in the Atlantic. When in Autumn 1940 he learned that Hitler intended to send training troops to Rumania he became furious because he considered Rumania to belong to the Italian sphere of interest. Out of this fury he decided to attack Greece in order to gain the Greek region of Epirus. On 28 October 1940 his troops began to attack.

The Italian attack on Epirus was stopped by the Greeks and soon they counterattacked and drove the Italians far back into Albania. In December 1940 the situation in Albania became so critical that he begged Hitler for help. Hitler, however, did not see a possibility to help Mussolini in winter. He had watched the Italian failure with sorrow because he feared that the British might intervene in Greece from where they might bomb the Rumanian oil fields which were decisive for German warfare. Moreover he was afraid of a British attack from the flank and the rear when he began his war against the Soviet Union, a war which he had planned since July. Therefore, on 13 November 1940 he released Führer Order (*Führerweisung*) no. 20 for operation *Marita,* the attack on Greece.

Five days later the Führer Order no. 21 for operation *Barbarossa* the attack on the Soviet Union was signed. This operation had been planned and prepared since July 1940. Both operations were now prepared in parallel. The opinion often heard in Greece that the attack and conquest of Greece delayed the attack on the Soviet Union by six weeks is a myth.[1] Besides, the preparations for both operations were in some parts identical. Rumania joined the Tripartite Pact (Germany, Italy, Japan) in November. During the next months bridges were built over the Danube and troops were moved into Rumania and on 1 March Bulgaria joined the Tripartite Pact and one day later the German troops entered Bulgaria. On 25 March the deployment of the 12th Army under field marshal Wilhelm List was finished and the troops were ready for the attack on Greece.

On 25 March Yugoslavia joined the Tripartite Pact. However on 27 March 1940 a British inspired coup took place in Belgrade. On the same day an enraged Hitler ordered the attack on Yugoslavia. (Führer Order no. 25). This coup abridged the Greek campaign because the strong Metaxas bunker line could be circumvented through Yugoslav territory. The attack began on 6 April 1941. On 9 April the Army Group Eastern Macedonia surrendered. On 27 April Athens was occupied. One day later the last British troops left Greece.

---

1 Heinz A. Richter, *Mythen und Legenden in der griechischen Zeitgeschichte* (Ruhpolding: Rutzen, 2016) , pp. 11-31.

The Greek soldiers had defended the Metaxas line so bravely, that Hitler allowed the whole Greek army to go home and that the officers could retain and carry their side arms. This gesture was acknowleged by the Greeks and if this had been the final decision there would have been, most probably, a peaceful occupation time. But now Hitler made a capital mistake. As he was of the opinion that he needed all troops for his campaign against the Soviet Union he assigned the occupation of Greece to the Italians and Bulgarians. They became the main occupation powers.

This decision was psychologically indeed an unbelievable capital mistake. The Greeks had defeated the Italians in Albania and they now became masters of the largest part of Greece as shown on the map on the next page. The Bulgarians were the hereditary enemies of Greece since the early 19th century. Now they were given the control over Thrace and immediately began to "Bulgarize" the province and in 1942 they annexed it.

The Greeks hated these two occupying forces. By the division of Greece into occupying zones the Germans forfeited the good will they had possessed before. They also became hated occupiers. Thus right at the beginning of the occupation the ground was laid for the future resistance of the people.

Now that the Italians were the main occupation force in Greece, even Athens was left to the Italians. Germany confined its control to the area of Dedeagatsch (Alexandroupolis), a strip of land along the Turkish border in order to avoid any clash there with the Turks. For strategic reasons the islands of Limnos, Lesvos, Chios and Samos were occupied by the Germans. Thessaloniki and hinterland became German as well. King Boris III of Bulgaria had demanded this town but Berlin had rejected this demand. Parts of Piraeus were also occupied by Germany. After the conquest of Crete two thirds of this island were under German and one third under Italian control.

History of Jewish Thessaloniki until WWII

The earliest Jewish community in Salonika came into being around 140 B.C. when Jews from Egypt settled there. Apostle Paulus visited the community and wrote a letter to them. Salonika belonged to the Roman and later to the Byzantine Empire. In 1430 the Ottoman Turks took over. Under the Romans the Jews enjoyed a wide autonomy which was limited when the Byzantines with their Christian state religion took over. Under Ottoman rule they shared the same freedom as all other religions with a book.

In the late Middle Ages Ashkenasi Jews arrived from Hungary and Germany and settled in Salonika. In the 16th century several thousands of Sephardic Jews arrived from Spain where they had been persecuted by the Inquisition and had fled to the Ottoman Empire and settled down in Thessaloniki. Most of them continued to speak their old-Castilian-Jewish dialect mixture (Ladino) and lived isolated from the Greek surroundings. In 1912 at the end of the Balkan wars Thessaloniki became Greek. This meant great changes.

In the Ottoman Empire Salonika had been an urban sea port with a vast hinterland providing very good economic consequences. Now it became a border city. Until 1912 the populations had consisted of Jews, Moslems (Turks and others) and Greeks. The Jews numbered 75,000 souls and shaped the character of the town.[1] Now all inhabitants became Greeks; thus the Jews were now Greek Jews. The process of Hellenization of the new area intensified after the defeat of Greece in the Greek-Turkish war (1919-1923) and the population exchange of the Lausanne Peace Treaty when over one million Greeks from Asia Minor streamed into the mother country, mainly into Macedonia.

Until 1912 the Jews had been the majority of Salonika's inhabitants. It had been a prosperous Jewish community of about 75,000 souls. Now they were Hellenized. Unfortunately, this process succeeded only with the younger generation. Until the eve of WWII only a small minority of the Jewish community spoke Greek. By law they were Greeks but their language and cultural differences and their closed society made them Jewish Greeks. They were a huge but isolated minority and their cemetery situated almost in the centre of the city was a thorn in the urban renewal and expansion. It was an obstacle for the growth of the city and therefore the Greeks wanted to transfer it to a place far outside the town. The town of Salonika proposed this repeatedly since 1925.[2] However, Jewish cemeteries cannot be moved and thus it became a stone of contention. Without outside interference a compromise might have been found but the occupation changed everything. The differences led to conflicts. The newspaper *Makedonia* permanently published anti-Semitic articles with the intention to deepen the differences. This led to a pogrom in the Camball quarter in 1931which in turn caused thousands of Jews to emigrate to Palestine. In 1932 the Greek state passed a law which obliged Jewish children to visit regular Greek schools. During the Metaxas dictatorship anti-Semitism was reduced but it remained under cover.[3]

1 Rena Molho, *Der Holocaust der griechischen Juden. Studien zur Geschichte und Erinnerung* (Bonn: Dietz, 2016), p. 57.

2 *Ibidem*, p. 63.

3 *Ibidem*, p. 58f.

The first occupation regime

On 9 June 1941 Hitler released Führer Order no. 31. It dealt with the chain of command in the Balkans. Wehrmacht Commander in Chief (Wehrmachtsbefehlshaber - W.B.) Southeast was Field Marshal Wilhelm List. He was subordinated directly to Hitler. He was the highest officer of the Wehrmacht in the Balkans and he held the executive power in all areas occupied by the Germans. He resided in Thessaloniki. Under his command were three subordinate commanders: The Commander of Serbia, the Commander of Saloniki-Ägäis and the Commander of Southern Greece. This structure remained in force until the end of December 1942.

Military Command Structures in the Balkans 1941-42

High Command of the Wehrmacht
Hitler
Commander in Chief South East
Wilhelm List (- Oct. 41)
Walter Kuntze (Oct. 41 - Jul. 42)

Commander Serbia	***Commander Saloniki-Ägäis***	***Commander Southern Greece***
	Curt v. Krenzki	Hellmuth Felmy (-Sept 42)
		Wilhelm Speidel (-Sept. 43)

Besides the military structure there existed a political one. On 28 April 1941 Hitler created the office of the "Bevollmächtigter des Reiches für Griechenland" (plenipotentiary of the Reich for Greece). It replaced the hitherto embassy and its head was the diplomat Dr. Günther Altenburg. His task was to negotiate with the Greek government over politics, economics and culture. In cases of military decisions which implied political aspects Altenburg had to be consulted as well. This caused of course friction and quarrels about the mutual competences.

Major General Curt von Krenzki was on the one hand commander of the troops which were still in Greece and on the other hand he was the bearer of the executive power. He was entitled to issue laws in the occupied area under his control. He could install special courts and give orders to the administration. These competences were based on article 43 of the Hague Convention. His decisions were announced to the public. An administrative staff existed parallel to the military staff. It belonged to the quartermaster's staff. The chief of the military administration of the WB Südost was Dr. Theodor Parisius. He was the superior of the three subordinated war administrative officers (Kriegsverwaltungsräte) in Serbia, Saloniki-Ägäis and Southern Greece. Parisius resided in Thessaloniki and so later did Merten.[1]

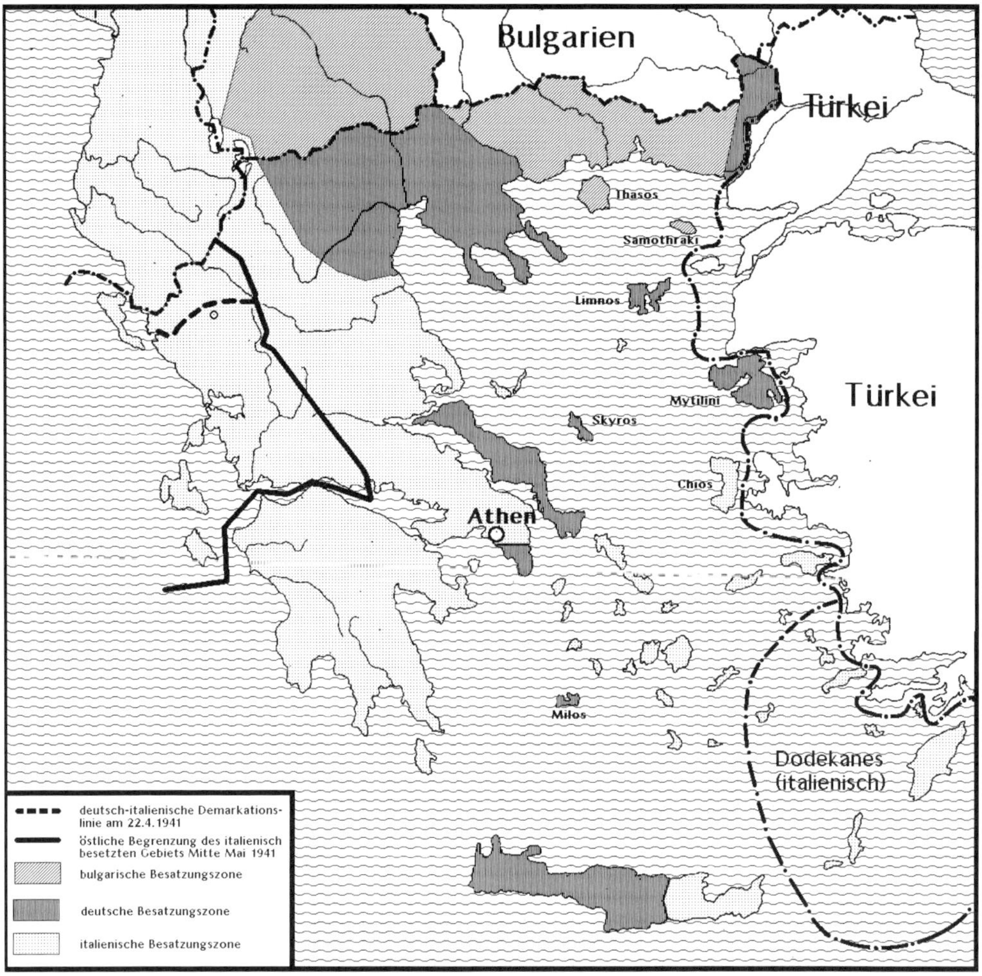

The Occupation Zones

The administrative officers were not part to the military hierarchy. They were civil servants in the service of the Wehrmacht. They did not have any military competence. Their tasks were: Finances, garment, catering, field equipment, postal service, travelling matters, control of food stores, military hospitals, accommodation of the troops and the administration of justice. And they were entitled to conscript civilians for compulsory labour according to the Hague Convention. A department of administration and economics existed

1 Breyer, *op. cit.*, p. 17f.

in the realm of the Commander Saloniki-Ägäis the head of which were Dr. Karl Marbach from June 1941 to July 1942 and Dr. Max Merten from August 1942 to March 1944. In other words: The administrative officers could never give any military orders let alone one concerning the shooting hostages.[1]

The Events of 11 July 1942 and the Expropriation of the Jewish Cemetery

In June 1941 the Rosenberg Task Force appeared in Salonika and confiscated the books of the libraries and the art treasures of the Jewish community and plundered the synagogues. The famine of winter 1941 hit the poor Jews worse than their Greek compatriots because these had peasant relatives in the countryside which the Jews did not have. Until early summer 1942 the German occupation forces left the Jews alone.

But now Wehrmacht authorities wanted to start building projects, mainly roads and reparations of railway lines. These projects would be accomplished by the Organization Todt (OT) which, of course needed local labourers. According to the Hague Convention such construction works had to be carried out by the authorities of the occupied state. In this case the responsible persons were the Governor General of Macedonia, Vasilis Simonidis, and the General Inspector of the Nomarchies of the Governor Generalship of Macedonia, a former General Athanasios Chrysochoou. Most historians, however, overlooked the first and made Chrysochoou Governor General.[2]

The first anti-Jewish measure had been an order by the local war administrative officer (Kriegsverwaltungsrat) Dr. Karl Marbach in April 1942 when he released an order which forbade four Jewish groups to travel to border areas under German control. Among them were former army officers and other young men who tried to get to the Near East to join the Greece forces there. Others tried to escape the famine of winter 1941.[3]

Karl Marbach was born in January 1909 in Wihelmshaven as son of an administrative officer. After finishing the classical grammar school (humanistiches Gymnasium) he studied law. During his studies he became a member of the Teutonia student corporation. In 1934 he was promoted to Dr. jur. by the University of Kiel. After the outbreak of the war he became administrative councillor of war (Kriegsverwaltungsrat).

In early summer 1942 the German command of Saloniki-Ägäis intended to repair roads and build new ones. According to the Hague Convention it was

1 *Ibidem*, p. 45 on the basis of a statement by Parisius.

2 Andrew Apostolou, "'The Exception of Salonika': Bystanders and Collaborators in Northern Greece" *Holocaust and Genocide Studies* 14:2 (2000), p. 176.

3 *Ibidem*, p. 177.

legal to make civilians, who were fit for work, build these roads. Therefore the local war administrative officer (Kriegsverwaltungsrat) Dr. Karl Marbach asked Simonidis to provide the work force necessary for these building measures. Simonidis said that he did not have the necessary financial means to do this. Instead he made an unbelievable proposal: He would draft several thousand of Jewish conscripts of certain age groups and they would perform this work without pay.[1]

Since Simonidis intended to conscript only Jews for this work, one might come to the obvious conclusion that he was a Greek anti-Semite, after all he did not intend to conscript Christian Greeks who were liable to military service. Marbach's lack of reaction on the other hand shows that he also was no friend of the Jews.

From 9 to 11 July 1942 the local newspapers *Apogevmatini* and the pro-Nazi paper *Nea Evropi* published an order which demanded that all Jews, between the age 18 and 45 years, belonging to the conscriptions years of birth from 1897 to 1924 appear in the *Plateia Eleftherias* (Freedom Square) at 8 o'clock in the morning to be registered. Those who would not appear risked punishment.[2]

At 8 o'clock on 11 July about 9,000 Jews assembled in the square. There under the supervision of Germans, officers and members of OT (Organisation Todt), Greek civil servants registered the Jews. The registered persons received a card with their name, profession, address and a serial number. Those who had fought in Albania and the civil servants of the town received a notice of exemption.[3] In 1960 *Der Spiegel* described the scene: *"While one after the other was registered and received his work pass the rest in the strength of a division spent its time with gymnastic exercises. The guards urged them on with whiplashes. Those who fainted on the shadeless freedom square got water poured over his head. The registered ones were allowed to leave - the first hundred meters crawling on their belly or doing sommersaults."*[4] In this ar-

---

1 *Ibidem*, p. 177; Hagen Fleischer, *Im Kreuzschatten der Mächte. Griechenland 1941-1944* (Frankfurt, Bern, New York: Peter Lang, 1986), p. 365 writes that it was Chrysochoou who made the proposal. Zentrale Stelle Ludwigsburg (ZStL)508 AR-Z139/59, Einstellungsverfügung der Staatsanwaltschaft Berlin vom 4.Juni 1968, Prozessgeschichte, p. 349

2 Michael Molho, *On Memoriam. Hommage aux Victimes Juives des Nazis en Grèce* (Salonique:1948), p. 42.

3 Rena Molho, *Der Holocaust der griechischen Juden. Studien zur Geschichte und Erinnerung* (Bonn: Dietz, 2016), p. 56.

4 *"Während einer nach dem anderen registriert und mit einem Arbeitsausweis versehen wurde, vertrieb sich der divisionsstarke Rest die Zeit mit gymnastischen Übungen. Die Wachen feuerten sie mit Peitschenschlägen an. Wer auf dem schattenlosen Freiheitsplatz ohnmächtig wurde, bekam Wasser über den Kopf. Die Registrierten durften sich entfernen*

ticle *Der Spiegel* seems to have taken over some typical Greek exaggerations and fabrications without further criticism. There exist dozens of photos showing the square filled with people. Some of them show squatting people but there is not one photo showing the terror described above.

The real excesses of the first day were in some cases so severe that the victims had to be treated by the Red Cross. Some of the Greeks who took part as clerks were unwilling aids of the Germans. A Greek who owned the house in which Krenzki resided complained about the events and Krenzki stopped the outrages.[1] The registration of the work force on 13 July then went on quietly. Rena Molho describes this as exceptional: Most Christian inhabitants of Salonika did not care about that what happened to the Jews.[2]

In the 1958 trial against Merten witnesses stated that they had seen him on the Square when the Jews were mistreated. Among them was general Archimidis Argyropoulos.[3] These statements were definitely wrong because Merten was still in Germany. He left Marburg in Germany on 3 August and arrived in Salonika on 10 August together with Parisius.[4] In another lawsuit in Berlin the prosecution stated: *"The witnesses who allegedly had seen Dr. Merten on the freedom square on 11 July 1942 must err. Possibly they mix different persons and events. A contributing factor might have been the fact that for all political and racial persecutions committed by the German occupation Dr. Merten the seemingly almighty leader of the military administration was held responsible."* Even the Greek special military court had found him not guilty in this point.[5]

During his trial in Athens Merten tried to get the help of his predecessor. On 22 July 1958 Marbach was asked by a member of the AA legal protection whether he had had any knowledge of German reprisals. Marbach denied this, though he had signed a document dealing with this problem on 3 November

---

- die ersten hundert Meter wahlweise auf dem Bauch robbend oder Purzelbäume schlagend." - "Griechenland: Ihr Onkel Konstantin" *Der Spiegel* 40 (28. September 1960), p. 30f. Similar report in *Hamburger Echo* (14. September 1960), p. 5.

1 ZStL 508 AR-Z139/59 Prozessgeschichte, p. 222.

2 Rena Molho, *op. cit.*, p. 55f.

3 Samuel Hassid,"The Trial of Max Merten in the Changing Mirros of Time and Place", in: http://greece.haifa.ac.il/events/holocaust_greece/Samuel_Hassid.pdf

4 ZStL 508 AR-Z139/59 Prozessgeschichte, p. 228f.

5 *"Die Zeugen, die Dr. Merten schon am 11. Juli 1942 auf dem Freiheitsplatz in Saloniki gesehen haben wollen, müssen sich irren. Möglicherweise bringen sie verschiedene Personen und Ereignisse durcheinander. Dazu könnte beigetragen haben, dass sie für die politischen und rassischen Verfolgungen, denen sie von Seiten der deutschen Besatzung ausgesetzt waren, ganz allgemein dem scheinbar allmächtigen Leiter der Militärverwaltung Dr. Merten verantwortlich gemacht haben." Ibidem*, p. 230.

1941.[1] Regarding Merten he stated that he had never met him. In truth he had cooperated some weeks with Merten after his arrival in Salonika on 10 August. Marbach even denied the events on 11 July on the Freedom Square in Salonika.[2] It was obvious that Marbach was not telling the truth even under oath.

About 3,500 Jewish conscripts were deployed in quarries and road building. Most of them could not physically cope with this hard work. Additionally they were badly fed and housed even worse. Many of them were forced to sleep in the open, they became ill and a great number of them died. According to Molho 60 percent of them were sick. The death rate was 12 percent. Their treatment by the German subcontractors of the OT was brutal.[3] One subcontractor was the Levantine Ioannis Miller who suggested on 20 August to the Jewish community that they should pay for hiring professional construction workers.[4]

The new war administrative officer Merten recognized that the Jewish forced labour was of little use. Then he heard about this proposal and took it over and intended to hire Greek professional road construction workers. However, this would be feasible if they received cash. After careful consideration on 13 October 1942 he contacted the leadership of the Jewish community and proposed to pay a transfer sum of 3,5 billion Drachmae and the forced labourers would be released. The Jewish community managed to collect 2 billion Drachmae (about 10,000 Sovereigns).[5] After renewed negotiations it was agreed that the remaining sum would be covered by the transfer of the Jewish cemetery to the city of Thessaloniki which had since long wanted the cemetery and would pay the rest of the sum. It is improbable that the newcomer Merten came up with the idea of the cemetery. It can be assumed that the proposal came from the interested Greek side.[6] Indeed Merten stated during this meeting: *"Many*

1 www.cia.gov/library Merten Case.pdf. *"Of the 488 executions which have taken place up to now, 442 took place during this reporting month."*

2 *Der Spiegel* 40 (28. September 1960).

3 Molho, *op. cit.*, pp. 44f, 47; ZStL 508 AR-Z139/59 Prozessgeschichte, p.223-228.

4 Leon Saltiel, "Dehumanazing the Dead. The Destruction of Thessaloniki's Jewish Cemetery in the Light of New Sources" *Akademia*, p.8.

5 According to the data of Neubacher in Oktober 1942 the price of one golden pound was 300.000 Drachmae thus it would have been 6,666 sovereigns. Hermann Neubacher, *Sonderauftrag Südost 1940-1945. Bericht eines fliegenden Diplomaten* (Seeheim: Buchkreis, 1966), p. 74.

6 Molho, *op. cit.*, p. 56.*"Depuis longtemps, certains protagonistes de la politique de clocher, férus d'un urbanisme d'occasion, voulaient obtenir la désaffectation du cimetière juif. Profitant de la présence des Nazis dans le pays, quelques uns d'entre eux, oublieux de toute pudeur et de toute délicatesse morale et patriotique, s'appuyèrent honteusement sur*

here are your enemies and they repeatedly lobby the German military administration for the destruction of the cemeteries and for the implementation of antisemitic measures."[1] Merten instructed Simonidis to make a proposal for a second substitute cemetery within a week.[2]

The Jewish community paid the sum and the forced labourers were set free. The cemetery was transferred to the town of Salonika. In December 1942 the graves were levelled and the tombstones destroyed or used as building material. Whether the the town paid the rest sum is not known but it can be assumed. The cemetery was transferred to the town and not to the Wehrmacht as one can often read. In the latter case it would have been restored to the Jewish community after the war. Today the university is located there.[3] On the connecting foot paths between the buildings one an still see the backside of tombstones used as paving stones.

On 8 December the Salonika newspaper *Apogevmatini* published an article on the transfer of the cemetery: *"The population of Thessaloniki felt relief with the news that, on the initiative of the German authorities, it was decided to transfer of the Jewish cemetery from the center of the city to its boundaries. Thanks to this decision, the area were the Jewish cemeteries are located today will soon be beautiful with expansion of the central park of the city to this point and with the erection of the public buildings envisioned by the city plan. [...] The people of Thessaloniki welcomed this initiative of the occupation authorities with gratitude."*[4]

Merten used the money as agreed to hire Greek workers.[5] The often read story that he stole the money is a straight forward lie. During Merten's trial the former head of the YDIP (*Υπηρεσία Διαχειρίσεως Ισραηλιτικών Περιουσιών*), Ilias Douros, denied that Merten pocketed the money.[6] Paul Isaak Haguel published reproductions of one of the seven checks and the reproduction

---

l'envahisseur, pour détruire précipitamment la vielle nécropole qui avait une valeur archéologique, historique, traditionnelle, sentimentale et artistique." Also AG Tiergarten 353 AR 1680/61, Anlage 1. The description of William Archer is rather prejudiced. William D. Archer, "The Merten Affair." MA Thesis (Sacramento: State University, 2016), p. 15f. *"The cemetery would be used for military purposes."*

1 Saltiel, *op. cit.*, p. 22
2 *Ibidem*, p. 8f.
3 Molho, *op. cit.*, pp. 48f, 56. The often heard claim that the Wehrmacht had intended to erect an ammunition depot on the cemetery is in view of the location of the cemetery absurd.
4 Saltiel, *op. cit.*, p.13.
5 ZStL 508 AR-Z139/59 Prozessgeschichte, p. 343.
6 Hassid, *op. cit.* In 1946 he had stated the opposite. The court threatened to persecute him for perjury.

shows clearly that the reproduced check was signed by Sabbetai Saltiel and countersigned by Merten and on 4 November 1942 it was deposited and paid in full to the Bank of Greece that same day.[1]

This fact is also accepted by Rena Molho. It is contrary to her earlier opinion, uttered on the same page, that the money was stolen and that Germany refuses to pay it back to the Jewish community.[2] This admission, however, does not hinder her to repeat the accusation a few pages later that Merten withdrew the money from the bank for his personal usage and that he, and not Marbach, ordered the forced labour of the Jews.[3] Merten, however, was still in Germany at that time.

In 1959 the court in Berlin came to the conclusion that when Merten made the Jewish community pay, it was a violation of international law. But Merten wanted to help the Jews and thus he had to choose between two evils. He could only fulfill his higher ranking ethical duty of saving the Jews by doing what he did.[4] Merten's main aim was to do his duty. He was a correct German civil servant. But at the same time he was a human being who wanted to help his fellow human beings.

All the time Simonidis had passed on German orders without any protest or delay. He seems to have sought to keep his own government in Athens in the dark. *"Simonidis was also repeatedly described as indifferent to the fate of the Jews. To German orders, however, Simeonidis was anything but indifferent, moving instead obediently and efficiently. Enepekidis describes him as trying to appear 'more German than the Germans', while Pierron had dubbed him 'a perfect example of a collaborator'."*[5]

During Merten's trial Chrysochoou stated *that "the destruction of the cemetery was celebrated as a huge benefit.[and] stirred emotions. [...] Christian representatives visited the German military commander to thank him on behalf of the city's Greek population for the definite solution of this issue."*[6] The anti-Semitism in the Greek population of Salonika accelerated the developments which had been in motion for decades but under the surface. The Germans made it to rise to the surface, they had the function of a catalyst.[7] Saltiel describes this development precisely: *"Two months before Eichman's men, Dieter Wisliceny and Alois Brunner arrived in Thessaloniki to execute the Fi-*

1 Paul Isaak Haguel, "History of the Jews of Thessaloniki and the Holocuast" ACADEMIA.
2 Rena Molho, *op. cit.*, p. 61.
3 *Ibidem*, p. 64.
4 ZStL 508 AR-Z139/59 Prozessgeschichte,, pp. 354, 359..
5 Apostolou, *op. cit.*, p. 179.
6 Saltiel, *op. cit.*, p. 22f.
7 *Ibidem*, p. 26.

nal Solution, the city's Jews saw their historic cemetery destroyed by a convergence of interests and ideology and a moral compass without orientation. The Jews lost their connection to their roots, just as they themselves were about to be uprooted. They were met with neglect, indifference, and - worse - hostility by the authorities, the same people who should have protected them during those difficult times. And as we now know, their fate had already been sealed."[1]

1 *Ibidem*, p. 27.

MERTEN AND THE PROSECUTION OF THE JEWS

The Arrival of Wisliceny and Brunner

In January 1943 the plenipotentiary of the Reich in Greece, Günther Altenburg, informed the Italian envoy in Athens that *SS Sturmbannführer* Rolf Günther would soon arrive in Salonika to remove the Jews of the city.[1]

On 6 February 1943 the final solution (Endlösung) of the Jewish question also began in Greece when *SS-Hauptsturmführer* Dieter Wisliceny and Alois Brunner arrived in Salonika on orders of the *Reichssicherheitshauptamt.* They were accompanied by a command of SD (*Sicherheitsdienst* - security service) consisting of 60 Sudeten Germans. Wisliceny carried an order of the *Reichssicherheitshauptamt* (SS-High Command) with him which said that the Nuremberg Race Law was to be applied in Greece as well. Merten called Dr. Willy Eckelberg of the Jewish department of the Reich's Ministry of the Interior and asked him whether this order of the SS was really binding. He explained that this would have negative consequences for the reputation of Germany and for the local war economy.. Eckelberg replied that he would have to consult the head of the department, Dr. Globke.

Globke's reply arrived a few days later. *"Globke could not imagine that I would not submit to an order coming from a central command. Whatever was in force in the area of the Reich [...] would be practised in occupied Greece as well. If the decision of the Reichssicherheitshauptamt had ordered that from now on the laws concerning the Jews of Germany should be applied. I had to apply them; besides that I should not care about things which were non of my business."*[2]

Wisliceny carried preformulated orders for the preparation of the *Endlösung* with him which had been applied in other countries before. On the same day Merten signed in the name of the *Befehlshaber Saloniki-Ägäis* the first of these orders which forced all Greek Jews to wear a yellow star and to live in a ghetto. Their shops should also be marked. Jews with a valid foreign passport were exempted. The execution of this order would be controlled by an

---

1 Apostolou, *op. cit.*, p. 179.

2 *"Globke könne sich nicht vorstellen, daß ich mich einem von einer zentralen Dienststelle kommenden Befehl nicht unterwerfen wollte. Was im Reichsgebiet gelte, müsse [...] auch im besetzten Griechenland praktiziert werden. Wenn die Entscheidung des Reichssicherheitshauptamtes dahin gegangen sei, daß nun in Griechenland nach den Judengesetzen des Reichsgebietes zu verfahren sei, so hätte ich das durchzuführen, außerdem solle ich mich nicht im Dinge kümmern, die mich nichts angingen." Hamburger Echo* (16. September 1960), p. 9.

SD-commando.[1] During the Athenian trial the former *Obermilitärverwaltungsrat* of army group E. Theodor Parisius, who had belonged to the superior office of Merten, stated that Merten signed this order with the knowledge of his commander.[2]

On 8 February 1943 Wisliceny called the chief rabbi Zvi Koretz. Koretz was born in 1884 in Rzeszów in Galicia. After studies in Berlin he became a rabbi. In 1933 the Jewish community of Thessaloniki elected him rabbi and in 1938 chief rabbi. At the end of 1942 he was made head of the community. It had been him with whom Merten had negotiated the deal about the cemetery. The community believed that because of his good knowledge of German Koretz would achieve the best for them. As he knew the Germans he was convinced that one could achieve the best by unconditional obedience and therefore he demanded from his community to obey the German orders. Thus he became a submissive tool of Wisliceny and Brunner.

On 12 February Wisliceny ordered the application of the Nuremberg laws.[3] After the establishment of the ghetto *Baron Hirsch,* Jewish security guards and policemen were appointed and other measures were taken to socially isolate the Jews. In March the Jewish possessions were confiscated. On 15 March the first and in May the last transport left Salonika. Until autumn 1943 46,091 Jews were transferred, most of them to Auschwitz-Birkenau. 95 percent of the Jewish population of Thessaloniki was killed.[4]

Already at that time Koretz was attacked because of his cooperation with the SD (Sicherheitsdienst - Security Service) and he was accused of not showving enough courage. He had done nothing to save his community from deportation and had blindly obeyed the orders of the SD. He had not understood anything and anticipated nothing. On 17 March when the transports to Poland had already begun he said in a synagogue in Salonika that all Jews would be transported to Poland where they could begin a new life among their fellow Jews. Koretz appealed to the rich to show solidarity with the poors because there had been rumours that only the poor would be deported. He left the synagogue under boos protected by the Jewish police.[5] Koretz himself was de-

1 Facsimile of this letter in Molho, *In Memoriam.*, p. 135. To these orders Merten ZStL 508 AR-Z139/59 Prozessgeschichte, p. 134f; AG Tiergarten 353 AR 1680/61, p, 14.

2 Botschaft an AA 503-88 No. 319/59 vom 26. Februar 1959, p. 2: AA Referat 206 Band Nr. 134.

3 Facsimile of Wisliceny's order in Molho, *In Memoriam* , p. 136f. A detailed description of the treatment of the Jews can be found in Heinz A. Richter, *Griechenland zwischen Revolution und Konterrevolution 1936 - 1946* (Frankfurt: Europäische Verlagsanstalt, 1973).

4 *Ibidem*, pp. 59-84.

5 *Ibidem*, p. 84.

ported in August 1943 together with his family and 74 members of the community and 367 Jews who had Spanish passports to Bergen Belsen as special detainees. He survived the war and died shortly after its end.

Since the orders were signed alternately by Merten and by Wisliceny the concerned persons and the Greek public gained the impression that Merten was responsible for the deportation of the Jews. It was not understood who was the initiator of the commands and that Merten was only part of a law enforcement agency. In Salonika the Wehrmacht in the person of the Befehlshaber Saloniki-Ägäis (til 31 December 1942 General Curt von Krenzki, then for two weeks General Bogislav von Studnitz and from 20 January 1943 on General Johannes Haarde) cooperated with the SS but the commanders were cautious enough not to expose themselves and let the lowest rank, Merten, do the dirty work. In the beginning Merten signed the first two orders: *"Für den Befehlshaber Saloniki-Ägäis. Der Chef des Stabes. Dr. Merten. Kriegsverwaltungsrat."* But from the third order on he signed by putting a "i. A. (im Auftrag - on order of - ooo in Nato-jargon) in front of his signature. This was the cautious attempt to distance himself from the sinister events. Wisliceny on the other hand signed with his name and "SS-Hauptsturmführer".[1]

Spiliotis interpreted Merten's *i. A.* as a proof of Merten's active participation in the deportation of the Jews. In order to prove this she quotes a statement by Eichmann during his trial in Israel: *"If Dr. Merten as deputy of the military commander had protested against the deportation Brunner could not have executed it because the primacy in all these questions lay with Dr. Merten as the deputy of the military commander. It is right [...] because [...] this same case can be applied in all occupied countries where there were military commanders. [...] If a military commander had vetoed it, even an order by Reichsführer [Himmler] could not have been executed."*[2]

---

1 Facsimiles *ibidem*, pp. 135-145. During his interrogation in Bratislava on 27 June 1947 Wisliceny alleged, that he had not signed one order. The prosecution in Berlin stated that Wisliceny tried to present Brunner and Merten as the main culprits, ZStL 508 AR-Z139/-59 Prozessgeschichte, p. 131.

2 *"Wenn Dr. Merten als Vertreter des Militärbefehlshabers gegen die Deportation protestiert hätte, hätte Brunner die Deportation nicht durchführen können, denn das Primat in allen diesen Fragen und die Befehlsgewalt lag bei Dr. Merten als Vertreter des Militärbefehlshabers. Es ist insofern richtig, ... weil [...] diese selbe Sache sich in allen Ländern gleichermaßen in Anwendung bringen läßt, ... wo Militärbefehlshaber waren, ... Hätte ein Militärbefehlshaber dagegen sein Veto eingelegt, [...] hätte auch ein Befehl des Reichsführers [Himmler...] dann in diesem Gebiet nicht durchgeführt werden können."* Susanne-Sophia Spiliotis, "Der Fall Merten, Athen 1959: Ein Kriegsverbrecherprozeß im Spannungsfeld von Wiedergutmachungs- und Wirtschaftspolitik" MA-Thesis (München,1991), p. 63.

Eichmann's statement is simply a lie. It was one of his attempts to justify his behaviour and to whitewash himself. Had Merten dared to refuse a signature he would have come into the greatest trouble. The Gestapo would certainly have arrested him and sent him to a concentration camp. A refusal to sign these orders would have required a readiness for martyrdom. Had the case been transferred to Krenzki nothing would have changed. Krenzki would have given in as did his comrades in Rhodos and Korfu who had also been threatened with Concentration Camp in a parallel case[1] Additionally Eichmann knew that Merten had incriminated him in his statements in Athens. Thus thisfriend he knew of the intention to exterminate the Jews. Mer statement was simply revenge. During Merten's trial general Chrysochoou stated clearly that Merten was not responsible but Krenzki.[2]

Efforts to Help the Jews

It is known that Merten constantly tried to save Jews as long as this did not endanger himself. In his trial he stated that he never made any false promises to the Jewish community. From a friend he knew of the intention to exterminate the Jews. Merten even tried to warn Rabbi Koretz but the Rabbi didn't believe him and prompted 5.000 Jews who had fled into the mountains to return.[3]

The Red Cross delegate, the Swiss Rene Burkhardt, confirmed that Merten did as much as possible to protect the Jews of Saloniki. When he learned that the SD commando would soon arrive he informed Burkhardt. The latter warned the chief rabbi Koretz who, however, did not react. But Burkhardt managed to induce some Jewish youths to flee.[4] When the SD commando arrived Merten told Burkhardt that from now on he could do nothing any more.[5] On 28 December 1946 Burkhardt wrote in his final report about his activities in Salonika to the then president of the International Red Cross, Carl Burkhardt, that Merten had given valuable help to the Red Cross. Contrary to the intention of Wisliceny he had delivered food to the Jews in the ghetto. *"Concluding I believe that Dr. Max Merten deserves a special treatment for his activities in*

---

1 Harald Gilbert, *Der Krieg in der Ägäis 1943-1944* (Wiesbaden: Harrassowitz, 2018), pp. 196-208.

2 *Ethnikos Kiryx* (18 February 1959): "O στρατιγός κ. Χρυσοχόου καταθέτει οτι ο Μερτεν ητο ξένος προς τους διωγμούς των Ισραηλιτών τα πάντα διετάσσοντο απο τον στρατηγόν Κρενσκυ."

3 Hassid, *op. cit.*.

4 Burkhardt to Staatsanwalt Bauer am 31. Januar 1961: Archiv für Christlich Demokratische Politik I-070-082/2.

5 AA Referat 206 Band 135: 8 JS 78/61 p. 74.

Salonika, especially for his hidden help to the Israelites and for his correct treatment."[1]

Burkhardt watched the deportation of the Jews and developed an idea how women and children could be saved by taking them to another country. On 29 May 1961 Merten testified the following in his hearing during the Eichmann trial: *"Each month one or two ships of the Red Cross arrived in Salonika which sailed back to Canada empty. Dr. Burkhardt wanted bring out the women and children on these ships. In March 1943 two ships came at the same time, so that there was a chance to bring out a number of ten thousand when they left."*[2]

Because the Swiss Consulate in Salonika had been closed in December 1942 Burkhardt contacted Merten.[3] The two agreed that Burkhardt would send a telegram to Merten. Merten would send this telegram via Dr. Günther Altenburg (Bevollmächtigter des Reiches in Griechenland) to the German Red Cross in Berlin asking to pass it on to the ICRC (International Committee of the Red Cross) in Geneva. As Merten did not trust Altenburg, because he closely cooperated with the SD, on 13 March he additionally sent the telegram directly to thc Rcd Cross in Berlin.[4] Merten later reported to the *Hamburger Echo* that he placed his teletype at Burkhardt's disposal who sent a message to the IRC in Geneva. The reply came immediately: "Approved",[5]it said.

The text of his own telegram read: *"Please telegraph to Inter-Red-Cross Center in Geneva: Start: Deportation of 45,000 Jews Salonki is almost decided. Stop. Urgent check with respective government deportation of women and children to Palestine necessary."*[6] On 17 March Altenburg contacted the

---

1 *"Zusammenfassend glaube ich persönlich, dass Dr. Max Merten von Seiten der Alliierten für seine Tätigkeit in Saloniki [...] eine Sonderbehandlung verdient, besonders was seine versteckte Hilfe an die Israeliten und seine korrekte Behandlung anbetraf."* Carl Burkhardt to Fredicia on 9 May 1961: Archiv für Christlich Demokratische Politik I-070-100/2 c.

2 *"Jeden Monat kamen ein oder zwei Dampfer des Roten Kreuzes nach Saloniki, die leer nach Canada zurückfuhren. Dr. Burkhardt wollte Frauen und Kinder mit diesen Dampfern herausbringen. Zufälligerweise kamen im März 1943 zwei Dampfer gleichzeitig an, so dass die Möglichkeit bestanden hätte, eine Zahl von zehntausend Personen bei dieser oder der nächsten Fahrt mitzunehmen."* Statement Merten: AG Tiergarten 353 AR 1680/61, p. 16. The existence of ths plan is verified by the Merci-diary. http://www.gemeinde.bozen.it/UploadDocs/6755_Merci_deutsch.pdf, p. 55.

3 Steven Bowman, "Another Righteous Gentile: The IRRC Representative in Salonika" *Thetis* 3 (1996), p. 219.

4 Aussage Merten: AG Tiergarten 353 AR 1680/61, p. 16.

5 *Hamburger Echo* (17.Septemner 1960), p. 10

6 *"Bitten Interrotkreuz Metropole Genf drahten ANFANG Deportation fünfundvierzig Tausend Juden Saloniki fast bestimmt STOP Dringliche Prüfung mit betreffenden Regie-*

representative of the ICRC in Athens, the Swiss Jean d'Amman, and made clear to him that the deportation of the Jews was a purely political matter which was of no concern for the ICRC. Burkhardt had transgressed his competence and had mingled in purely German affairs. Burkhardt had to leave Greece but this should be done in a discreet way. D'Amman called Burkhardt and informed him. Burkhardt agreed but he would leave only after an adequate substitute had arrived. This change, however, took three months.[1] But without Merten's help the telegram would never have arrived in Geneva.

In his testimony in the Eichmann case Merten stated that Eichmann had called him in Salonika. He remonstrated with him on the Jewish question and asked him since when he was emigration commissioner and that his interference impeded Wisliceny's work. Merten countered that the evacuation would disturb the civilian population and irritate the International Red Cross. He suggested to Eichmann that he would come to Berlin and talk to him in person. Eichmann agreed and Merten obtained the permission of General Krenzki to travel to Berlin.[2]

Merten took the train and travelled via Budapest, where he met his wife who lived there in the house of her parents, to Berlin. During a conversation which lasted one and a half hours Merten succeeded to convince Eichman of his proposal whch Eichmann accepted. On the basis of an article in the newspaper *Hamburger Echo Der Spiegel* wrote that Merten told Eichmann that it would be more reasonable to transport as many Jews as possible to Palestine instead of using the scarce number of rail waggons for their transport to Auschwitz. *"Eichmann asked me 'how many'. I answered: 'Well around 10,000.' Eichmann: 'Take 20,000.' Main thing, we get rid of them.' In my presence Eichmann stuck up towards Globke for the life of 20,000 Jews. In vain [...] Eichmann made the impression of a caged tiger. Repeatedly he yelled 'This Globke ... The Führer has ordered. More he did not risk to say,"* Eichmann had tried to reassure himself by talking to Globke. Allegedly Eichmann per-

---

rungen Deportation Frauen und Kinder Palestina erforderlich." Text in AG Tiergarten 353 AR 1680/61 Anlage 9 und Jean-Claude Favez, *Une mission impossible? Le CICR, les déportations et les camps de concentrations nazi* (Lausanne, 1988), p. 254. The text of the telegram reads: Please send telegram to International Red Cros in Geneva: The deportation of 45,000 Jews from Salonka almost certain. Urgently check with the relevant governments whether deportation of women and children to Palestine is possible."

1 Bowman, *op. cit.*, p. 219.

2 Aussage Merten: AG Tiergarten 353 AR 1680/61, p. 16f; Breyer, *op. cit.*, p. 82. According to the *Hamburger Echo Eichmann said; "Sind Sie verrückt geworden, Merten! Sie wisse doch, dass auf Hochverrat die Todestrafe steht?" Hamburger Echo* (17. September 1960), p. 10.

mitted Merten to transfer these 20,000 Jews to Palestine on his own initiative:[1] *"Then Eichmann suddenly stopped: 'Well, Merten, if you like these sh..-Jews so much, then do the thing nevertheless. If Wisliceny complains he must complain to me. And I will see to it that it will be ok."*[2] The latter statement is convincing since Eichmann was superior to Wisliceny. Merten, on the other hand, showed an astonishing amount of courage trying to help the Jews.

However, in Berlin Globke objected. After his return to Salonika Merten tried twice to contact the British via the IRC. But now the British side refused to accept the transport. Lord Moyne who was responsible for the British mandated territory of Palestine had refused to let such a great number of Jews enter the country. They would provoke disturbances. Therefore the relief operation could not take place.[3] In November 1944 Lord Moyne was assassinated by the Jewish terrorist group. Later on his refusal served as a cover up of Globke's guilt.

The question arises for the competence of Globke to stop this action? To answer this question one must go back to the year 1935 when the Nuremberg racial laws were proclaimed on 15 September. Globke was one of the chief commentators of that law. The content of the commentaries prove that he was a radical Catholic anti-Semite.[4] In the years after the war he and others tried to get away with the contention that they had done their best to lessen the consequences of the laws. This was an effort to hide their own complicity. In reality Globke was one of those who evacerbated the laws. While Wilhelm Stuckart who was undersecretary of State in the Interior Ministry and participant of the Wannsee-Conference in 1942 wrote the introduction, it was Globke who wrote the numerous pages of commentary. He especially sharpened the pa-

---

1 *"Eichman fragte mich 'wieviel'. Darauf ich: 'Na rund 10.000.' Eichmann: 'Nehmen Sie 20.000. Hauptsache, wir sind sie los.' So hat sich Eichmann in meiner Gegenwart gegenüber Globke für das Leben von 20.000 Juden stark gemacht. Umsonst. [...] 'Eichmann machte den Eindruck eines eingesperrten Tigers. Immer wieder brüllte er: 'Dieser Globke ... Der Führer hat doch befohlen ... Mehr traute der sich nicht zu sagen."* Aussage Merten: AG Tiergarten 353 AR 1680/61, p. 17. "Griechenland: Ihr Onkel Konstantin" *Der Spiegel* 40 (28. September 1960), Steven Bowman, "Another Righteous Gentile: The ICRC Representative in Salonika" *Thetis*3 (1996), pp. 217-220; Breyer, *op. cit.*, p. 81f. P. St., "Max Merten contra Hans Globke" *Die Zeit* 45 (1965).

2 *"Dann hielt Eichmann plötzlich inne: 'Na schön, Merten, wenn Sie an den Scheißjuden so sehr hängen, dann machen Sie die Sache trotzdem. Und sollte sich Wisliceny beschweren, so muß er sich bei mir beschweren. Und ich werde schon aufpassen, daß das in Ordnung geht!" Hamburger Echo* (17. September 1960), p. 10.

3 Aussage Merten: AG Tiergarten 353 AR 1680/61, pp. 16-19. "Kriegsverbrechen Griechenland. Ihr Onkel Konstantin" *Der Spiegel* 40 (28. September 1960), p. 32.

4 Fritz Bauer Archiv, *Der Fall Dr. Hans Globke.*

ragraph which dealt with "Rassenschande" (sexual intercourse with a member of a "race inferior to the one he belongs to"). During the war Globke was the official who was concerned with the the Jewish matters in the Ministry of the Interior of the Reich.

MdB (Member of Bundestag) of the SPD (Social Democratic Party) Adolf Arndt, who in 1933 had been fired as a judge for racial reasons, stated in 1950 in Parliament: *"Who as a jurist scholarly comments such a deed or misdeed as the Nuremberg Laws are exposes himself to the accusation that what he wrote cannot be called anything else than judicial prostitution."* Another statement is even more pronounced calling Globke a "Schreibtischtäter" (white-collar criminal).[1] Globke was also the author of the law which demanded from Jews to have the second first name Israel or Sara entered to their passport.

During the war Globke continued to work in the ministry of the interior. His task now was the application of the Nuremberg Laws in the occupied countries. Details are not known. On what basis he could interfere in the question of the transport of the Jews to Palestine is not known but we will come back to him in a later chapter. After the war Globe managed to avoid punishment by getting so-called "Persilscheine" (Certificate of good conduct) from former colleagues. After the foundation of the FRG he became undersecretary of state in the office of Chancellor Adenauer.

However, there is more evidence that Merten helped the Jews. During the Athens trial the former Italian consul, Guiseppe Castrucci, gave testimony in favour of Merten. He, the consul, had tried to save the Jews from the grip of the SS by taking them to Athens in the Italian zone of occupation. For this purpose he had issued Italian passports to the Jews. In July 1943 an Italian military train had gone from Salonika to Athens with more than 300 Jews. *"Without Merten's help this saving of the Jews would have been impossible because Merten allowed the train with the Jews to move though he knew that the Italian passport did not belong to them and the Gestapo was deceived."* Professor Lucilo Merci who had been interpreter in the Italian General Consulate said in the Athens court that with the help of Mertens at first 113 and

1 *"Wer als Jurist eine solche Tat oder Untat, wie es die Nürnberger Gesetze sind, scheinbar wissenschaftlich kommentiert, setzt sich dem Vorwurf aus, dass das, was er dort geschrieben hat, kaum mit einer anderen Bezeichnung versehen werden kann, als der einer juristischen Prostitution."* Jürgen Bevers, *Der Mann hinter Adenauer. Hans Globkes Aufstieg vom NS-Juristen zur Grauen Eminenz der Bonner Republik* (Berlin: Christoph Links, 2009), p. 36.

later 350 Jews were saved out of the Jewish camp by train transport to Athens. An affidavit of the Jewish community confirmed this in 1946.[1]

During the first months of the deportations it was the Italian General Consul Guelfo Zamboni who freed "Italians" from of the Baron von Hirsch ghetto.[2] Merten's lawyer, Matsoukas, stated in his final defence speech that in the first bill of indictment Merten had not been accused of having participated in the deportation of the Jews.[3] Wolfgang Breyer published more cases in his dissertation how Merten helped Greeks and Greek Jews.[4] But not only the Italians helped the Jews. The Norwegian, Dutch, Spanish and the Iranian consuls took over Jews en bloc, which Merten could cross out from the deportation list. Allegedly their number was 13,000.[5]

Attached to Merten's office was a large office of translators in which many graduates of the German school of Salonika worked. In 2000 Breyer succeeded in contacting one of them, a certain Juli B. Pierbonis. She spoke very positively about Merten and reported that he had had a gifted young man as right hand who was an Austrian Jew. Unfortunately he died a year later of eye tuberculosis. Another graduate of the German school who became later the wife of the Heidelberg university professor of archaeology Jörg Schäfer, and who had also worked in Merten's office, also spoke very positively about Merten. She remembered the name of Merten's right hand: Alexander Asseo. Pierbonis told that Asseo's mother stemmed from the famous Austrian musician family of Gelber. After the Germans occupied Greece the Asseo family changed its name to Astos which sounded less suspicious to German ears. Merten allegedly saved the famous Greek actor Manos Katrakis from death by starvation.[6] Katrakis later joined EAM/ELAS and during the civil war he was interned in Makronissos.

---

1 *"Ohne Unterstützung von Merten wäre diese Rettung der Juden nicht möglich gewesen, denn Merten habe den Zug mit den Juden fahren lassen, obgleich er gewusst habe, dass ihnen die italienischen Pässe nicht zustanden und die Gestapo dadurch getäuscht wurde."* Botschaft an AA 503-88 No. 319/59 vom 26. Februar 1959, p. 4: AA Referat 206 Band Nr. 134; Merci wrote a diary: http://www.gemeinde.bozen.it/UploadDocs/6755_Merci_-deutsch.pdf. According to the diary Merten saved 436 persons. Merci wrote further that Merten (p. 46), signed the permits of the Jews so they could pass unhindered. Hassid, *op. cit.*. The story reported by Archer, *op. cit.*, p. 27 is rather implausible. Merten would scarcely have been ready to do the work of a policeman.

2 Tagebuch Merci p. 40.

3 Botschaft an AA 503-88 No. 319/59 vom 26. Februar 1959, p. 2: AA Referat 206 Band Nr. 134.

4 Breyer, *op. cit.*, pp. 117-120.

5 *Hamburger Echo* (16. September 1969), p. 9.

6 Breyer, *op. cit*, p. 55.

Alleged Shooting of Hostages and Executions

Another point of the indictment in the trial against Merten was his alleged reprisals against the civil population. He was accused of having shot many prisoners and hostages. In order to clear this matter the central legal protection department of the AA (ZRS) made an effort to explain the command structures. From August 1942 to the end of the year there had been a Wehrmachtsbefehlshaber Südost (Alexander Löhr) based in Thessaloniki. In January 1943 this was changed into OB (Oberbefehlshaber) Südost and Army Group E. The OB Südost had the same competences as he WB Südost. The OB Südost was commander of the Army Group E in personal union. Under the OB Südost's orders were the Befehlshaber Saloniki-Ägäis (since 20 January 1943 Johannes Haarde) and the Befehlshaber Südgriechenland (Wilhelm Speidel). Both were responsible for the administration of occupied Greece. The office of the Befehlshaber Saloniki-Ägäis carried the rank of an upper field command (Oberfeldkommandatur). Merten was under his command.[1]

The ZRS asked the former chief of staff of the army group E and Commander Southern Greece Speidel to contribute their knowledge to the case. Speidel who had been sentenced to jail by the 6th Nuremberg trial replied sarcastically that he "an experienced war criminal" was ready to make Merten's fate easier. He wrote a paper on the military assignments but refused that this paper would be presented in Athens. He wondered why these stories would be warmed up again.[2] Indeed Speidel was no war criminal.

In the Athens trial the former administrative officer Parisius stated that *"a Kriegsverwaltungsrat did not have any executive competence or authority to give directives to units of the Wehrmacht or police.. [...] On the question of the shooting of hostages Parisius explained in detail while stressing the limited competence of the military administration that Merten according to his competence had nothing to do with this."* The former General Gerhard Engel supported this and then wrote about the "relocation" of the Jews: On 2 November 1941 Hitler gave Himmler a special authority *"to relocate the Jews with a SS-special command, but ordered that the military commander Saloniki Ägäis should involved only it is absolutely necessary."* He was to be informed but at the same time be told not to disturb these measures under no circumstances.[3] Parisius and Engel further stated that *"the anti-Jewish measure lea*

---

1 Richter, *Revolution*, p. 193.

2 Spiliotis, *op. cit.*, p. 97. She caracterized Speidel's remark as cynical.

3 *"ein Kriegsverwaltungsrat keinerlei Exekutivbefugnisse oder Weisungsrechte an Einheiten der Wehrmacht oder Polizei gehabt habe. [...] Zu der Frage der Geiselerschießungen leg-*

ding to the expulsion of Salonika's Jews were the responsibility of Wisliceny and Brunner and their people - and not Merten."[1]

The prosecution had accused Merten of having participated in the shooting of 680 Greek hostages or to have ordered these shootings. The testimonies of Parisius and Engel, both former officers, impressed the military judges so much that they discharged Merten in this case. Especially Engel impressed the Greek military: *"When Engel answered to a question that he had served in the infantry, one of the military assessors said smilingly in German: 'We are comrades'."*[2]

In another case the court accused Merten that he had allegedly ordered the shooting of five Jews among them two children and sentenced him to 18 years in prison [3] The prosecution in Berlin which also examined the case doubted that Merten had had the authority to order the shooting and stated that two adults (Albert Benveniste and Nissim Kamhi) were shot on the order of an unknown person. Regarding the children they found out that there was an error of names, they were not related to the adults. The Berlin prosecution could not find any guilt with Merten.[4]

Therefore it can be stated here, that Merten was not involved in the shooting of hostages or in any executions. His job was of the administrative kind only and not of the military kind. He was a civil servant in the service of the Wehrmacht and as such he was not involved in any executions. Marbach, however, was demoted to the rank of a sergeant and sent to the Eastern Front. There he contracted poliomyelitis and from then on he was bound to a wheelchair until he died in 1974.

---

te Parisius unter Hervorhebung der begrenzten Befugnisse der Militärverwaltung eingehend dar, dass Merten seiner ganzen Zuständigkeit nach hiermit nichts zu tun gehabt habe." - "die Umsiedlung mit einem SS-Sonderkommando durchzuführen, dabei aber ausdrücklich befohlen, dass der Militärbefehlshaber Saloniki nur soweit dringend erforderlich einzuschalten sei." Botschaft an AA 503-88 No. 319/59 vom 26. Februar 1959, p. 1: AA Referat 206 Band Nr. 134.

1 Hassid, *op. cit.*

2 Botschaft an AA 503-88 No. 381/1959 Anlage vom 6. März 1959; AA Referat 206 Band Nr. 135.

3 *"Als Engel auf Befragen erklärte, er habe bei der Infanterie gedient, sagte einer der militärischen Beisitzer lächelnd auf Deutsch: 'Wir sind Kameraden'." Ibidem*; Breyer, *op. cit..*, p. 65.

4 Ludwigsburg ZStL 508 AR-Z139/59 Prozessgeschichte, pp. 203-215.

The Confiscation of Jewish Property

As in Germany the property of the Jews was confiscated in Greece as well. On 20 February 1943 the Jews were forbidden to sell their possessions. From the same day on troops of Greek citizens under the lead of SD special commandos and of an agent by name of Laskaris Papanaoum were on their way to confiscate all Jewish shops and to seal them.[1] On 7 March an order was released by Merten (MV pol 5 2839 Dr. Me), signed i. A., which also stemmed from Wisliceny which demanded that trustees should be appointed for all Jewish shops and handicraft enterprises. For their supervision an office for the administration of the Jewish fortunes (*Υπηρεσία Διαχειρίσεως Ισραηλιτικών Περιουσιών*, YDIP) would be established. The Governor General of Macedonia controlled this real estate office of Thessaloniki. In the middle of March Wisliceny informed the YDIP that the Jewish possessions would be transferred to the Greek state. On 20 May Merten published the according order signing I. A.. It read: The existing Jewish property in the realm of the *Militärkommandantur Saloniki-Ägäis* will be transferred to the Greek state. The trustees which were appointed by the Governor General [Simonidis] could freely dispose of it. The shops should continue their work. Under German control 300 trustees were appointed.[2] During Merten's trial the former chief of the YDIP, Ilias Douros, stated that Merten did not benefit from from the looting of the Jewish property. *"His services consisted of writing formal contracts for the transfer of Jewish property to new owners."*[3]

Merten's part in the appointment of the trustees was rather small. The main work was done by the *Militärverwaltungsinspektor* Eberhard Kuhn, a direct subordinate of Merten. Merten's chief interpreter Arthur Meißner was involved as well.[4]

Breyer, however, described in his thesis a great number of cases where Jewish enterprises were transferred to private citizens. There were cases where relatives or acquaintances of Greek collaborators, e.g. Papanaoum were the beneficiaries. Informers were also entitled to Jewish possessions. The Governor General distributed the empty Jewish apartments [5] It can be assumed that

1 *Ibidem*, p. 241f.
2 *Ibidem*, pp. 242-248.
3 Hassid, *op. cit.*
4 Ludwigsburg ZStL 508 AR-Z139/59 Prozessgeschichte, p. 319.
5 Thus Breyer, *op. cit.*, pp. 68-74, 76-78. Also Stratos Dordanas and Vaios Kalogrias, "Die jüdische Gemeinde von Thessaloniki während der deutschen Besatzungszeit 1941-1944: Zwischengemeindliche Beziehungen, Ghettoisierung und Deportation" *PaRDeS Zeitschrift der Vereinigung für Jüdische Studien* 17 (Potsdam, 2011), p. 114.

great parts of the Jewish property were "hellenized" and remained so, similarly to the aryanized property in post-war Germany.

On 13 March Merten released another order of Wisliceny which on 15 March was followed by one of Wisliceny by which the Jews of Thessaloniki were requested to transfer their liquid funds and their articles of value to the Jewish community, i.e. the occupation forces. In case of non-compliance punishment threatened.[1] Allegedly 280 billion Drachmae were collected. This sounds impressive, but in view of the galloping inflation at that time it was not more than the sum which was paid for the release of the forced labourers. After the war Wisliceny claimed before the IMT (International Military Tribunal) that the collected money was taken over by the military administration. Merten said that the collected jewellery was sent to the Embassy in Athens and from there by air transport to Germany. The latter coincides with an order by Goering of 5 November 1941 which ruled that all precious metal and jewellery should be delivered to the central treasury of the Reich.[2] It cannot be assumed that greater parts of these "disappeared."

All this took place under the eyes of Simonidis. He did not intervene once. He and Chrysochoou observed any Bulgarian transgression diligently but in the case of the Jews they looked the other way. Apostolou suspects him that he used the opportunity offer by the SS to complete the Hellenization of Salonika. Therefore he let the SS do the dirty work.[3]

Allegedly the valuable furniture of the deported Jews was taken to Germany and given to bombed out people but the furniture did not become Merten's privat property. The accusation that Merten enriched himself with the fortunes of the Jews cannot be proven.

In Greece a myth is still circulating, i.e. the myth that the gold which Neubacher used to stabilize the highly inflationary Greek Drachmae was the gold of the Jews. Allegedly 12 tons of gold were confiscated which would have corresponded with 1,5 million golden sovereigns. This myth is still alive because nobody is ready to believe that during the war Nazi-Germany paid 1 million golden coins to stabilize the Drachmae. This myth, however, found its way into an article of the *Frankfurter Allgemeine Sonntagszeitung* in 2015.[4] The money collected from the Jews were Drachmae and their value was about 10,000 sovereigns. Neubacher's gold stemmed exclusively from the Reichs-

1 ZStL 508 AR-Z139/59 Prozessgeschichte, p. 299.
2 *Ibidem*, p. 302.
3 Apostolou, *op. cit.*, pp. 180f, 186..
4 Burger, *op. cit.*, p. 1.

bank and the one million golden coins comprised French golden Francs (about 60 percent) and 40 percent Sovereigns.[1]

Neubacher's gold action stabilized the Drachmae until the Germans withdrawal. After the German retreat the inflation reached astronomical proportions. In October 1944 one sovereign cost 1.3 billion Drachmae. All existing Greek money could have been had for 100,000 pounds. The inflation reached such a dimension that the Drachmae lost its character as money. The British currency specialist David Waley ordered a currency devaluation in 1945. 29 billion old Drachmae became one new Drachmae. This improved the situation considerably but it took quite some time until the inflation really ended.[2]

Two weeks after the return of the government in exile of Papandreou in October 1944 it decided to return the Jewish assets but this did not work. When in summer 1945 the first survivors of the concentration camps returned they found the trustees of the occupation regime in their houses. Besides that many homeless people had occupied the empty houses and this situation would worsen during the civil war. The improved restitution law of 1945 was ratified only in 1949 after the end of the civil war and only under the pressure of the US and the World Jewish Congress.[3]

Another example may show what really happened. After the war the son of a Jew who had been killed in Auschwitz wanted back the shop of his father from the trustee. When the trustee refused the restitution the son had to go to court. The court decided that the son should submit the certificate of death of his father from Auschwitz. As this was impossible the trustee could keep the shop. If a shop was returned then it would be empty. Heirs had great difficulties getting their heritage back. Of course there were correct retro-transfers but these were not the rule. Therefore there were beneficiaries of the holocaust in Greece as well.[4]

Because Merten was involved in the handling of the confiscated Jewish properties the Greek side insinuated that he had enriched himself and had collected huge treasures. Allegedly he took a small part to his wife who lived in Hungary at that time and hid a greater part somewhere in Greece. This ru-

---

1 Heinz A. Richter, *Mythen und Legenden in der griechischen Zeitgeschichte* (Mainz: Rutzen, 2016), pp.109-111.

2 Heinz A. Richter, *Geschichte Griechenlands im 20. Jahrhundert, II, 1939-2004* (Ruhpolding: Rutzen, 2015), pp. 194, 210.

3 Hagen Fleischer, "Saloniki unter dem Hakenkreuz" Vortrag (Thessaloniki, 15. März 2011).

4 Mitteilungen von Samuel Hassid in mehreren E-Mails an den Verfasser im Juli 2012. About this also Rena Molho, *op. cit.*, pp. 78-87. Also Götz Aly, *Europa gegen die Juden 1880-1945* (Frankfurt: S. Fischer, 2017), p. 27.

mour circulated in Greece for decades as I personally remember but nobody took it seriously. However in I999 this rumour assumed an unbelievable reality. This story will be described in a later chapter.

Merten's Last Months in Salonika

As we already stated Karl Marbach had been war administrative officer from June 1941 to July 1942. Merten arrived in August 1943 and remained in Salonika until March 1943. He had then to leave Salonika because of a legal attack by the German military judiciary accusing him of favouring the Greeks. His successor was Dr. Markull who stayed in Salonika from April to July 1944. His successor was Müller-Osten from July to the end of the occupation. Merten was transferred to Montenegro, then to Belgrad and Tirana. In August 1944 he was ordered to go to Zagreb where he served on the staff of the quartermaster of Army Group E until the end of the war. Until the end of 1946 he was a prisoner of war of the Americans and then a civilian internee in Dachau because of his administrative activity in Greece.[1]

1 Breyer, *op. cit.*, p. 12f; Testimony of Merten to Amtsgericht Tiergarten Abt. 353 AR1680/61 on 29 Mai 1961.

Fig. 1 The Jews on the Plateia Eleftherias on 11 June 1942

Fig. 2 "Sporting exercises" on Plateia Eleftherias

Fig. 3 "Sporting exercises" on Plateia Eleftherias

Fig. 4 "Sporting exercises" on 22 July 1942

Fig. 5 Jewish Cemetery in Salonika - in the background the White Tower

Fig.6 The Jewish Cemetery in Salonika

Fig. 7 Footpath out of Tomb Stones

Fig. 8 Jewish Women before the Deportation

Fig. 9 Dieter Wisliceny

Fig. 10 Alois Brunner

Fig. 11 Lord Moyne

Fig. 12 Hans Globke

Fig. 13 A Mount Athos Monastery

Fig. 14 Kriegsverwaltungsrat Merkull on Mount Athos

Fig. 15 Christmas on Mount Athos 1943

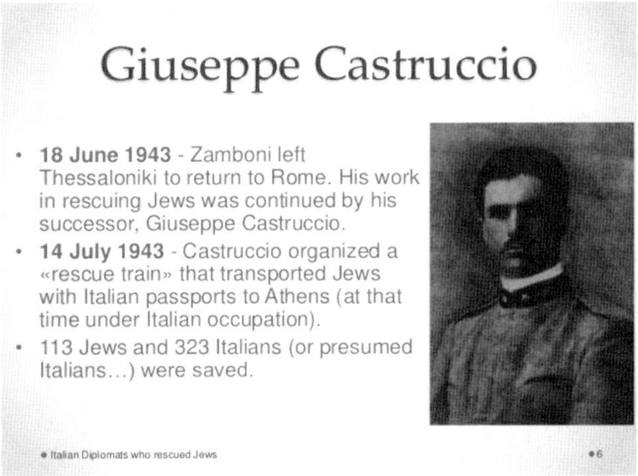

Fig. 16 Giuseppe Castrucio

Fig. 17 Lucillo Merci

Fig. 18 Merten in the Athens Court in 1957

Fig. 19 Portrait of Max Merten in 1935

Fig. 20 Max Merten in the 1950ies

Fig. 21 Merten and his Team

Fig. 22 The Merten Family in the 1950ies

Fig. 23 Prosecutor Andreas Tousis

Fog. 24 Dimitrios Makris

Fig. 25 Merten in Court

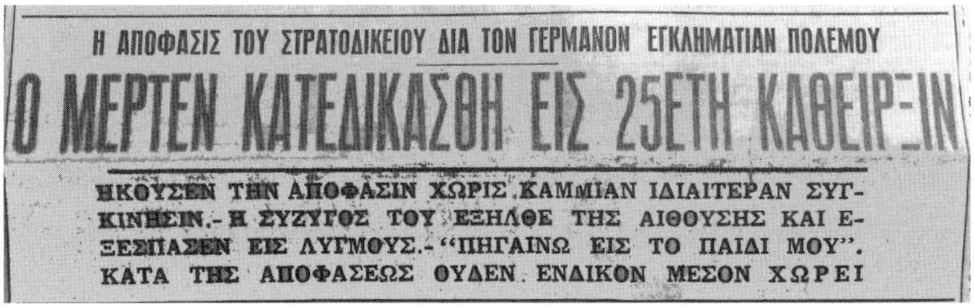

Η ΑΠΟΦΑΣΙΣ ΤΟΥ ΣΤΡΑΤΟΔΙΚΕΙΟΥ ΔΙΑ ΤΟΝ ΓΕΡΜΑΝΟΝ ΕΓΚΛΗΜΑΤΙΑΝ ΠΟΛΕΜΟΥ

Ο ΜΕΡΤΕΝ ΚΑΤΕΔΙΚΑΣΘΗ ΕΙΣ 25ΕΤΗ ΚΑΘΕΙΡΞΙΝ

ΗΚΟΥΣΕΝ ΤΗΝ ΑΠΟΦΑΣΙΝ ΧΩΡΙΣ ΚΑΜΜΙΑΝ ΙΔΙΑΙΤΕΡΑΝ ΣΥΓ-
ΚΙΝΗΣΙΝ.- Η ΣΥΖΥΓΟΣ ΤΟΥ ΕΞΗΛΘΕ ΤΗΣ ΑΙΘΟΥΣΗΣ ΚΑΙ Ε-
ΞΕΣΠΑΣΕΝ ΕΙΣ ΛΥΓΜΟΥΣ.- "ΠΗΓΑΙΝΩ ΕΙΣ ΤΟ ΠΑΙΔΙ ΜΟΥ".
ΚΑΤΑ ΤΗΣ ΑΠΟΦΑΣΕΩΣ ΟΥΔΕΝ ΕΝΔΙΚΟΝ ΜΕΣΟΝ ΧΩΡΕΙ

Fig. 26 Headline: Merten convicted to 25 years prison

Η ΤΕΛΕΥΤΑΙΑ ΗΜΕΡΑ ΤΗΣ ΔΙΚΗΣ ΤΟΥ ΜΕΡΤΕΝ

Ὁ Γερμανὸς ἐγκληματίας πολέμου Μὰξ Μέρτεν κατὰ τὴν χθεσινὴν συνεδρίασιν τοῦ Στρατοδικείου, τὸ ὁποῖον τὸν κατεδίκασεν εἰς 25 ἐτῶν εἱρκτήν. Δεξιά, διακρίνεται ἡ σύζυγος τοῦ Μέρτεν, ἡ ὁποία ἀφίχθη ἐκ Γερμανίας διὰ νὰ παρακολουθήσῃ τὴν δίκην.

Fig 27 The last Day in Court: Merten, lawyer Matsoukas and on the right Merten's Wife

ΚΑΤ' ΕΦΑΡΜΟΓΗΝ ΤΟΥ ΔΙΑΤΑΓΜΑΤΟΣ ΥΠΕΡ ΤΩΝ ΕΓΚΛΗΜΑΤΙΩΝ ΠΟΛΕΜΟΥ

Ο ΜΕΡΤΕΝ ΑΝΕΧΩΡΗΣΕ ΧΘΈΣ ΕΙΣ ΓΕΡΜΑΝΙΑΝ

Τὸ ἀεροπλάνον τοῦ ὁποίου ἐπέβη ἐπέστρεψεν κατόπιν τηλεφωνήματος ὅτι θὰ ἀνετινάσσετο ἀπὸ βόμβαν

ΑΝΕΧΩΡΗΣΕΝ ΟΡΙΣΤΙΚΩΣ ΜΕΤΑ ΤΕΤΡΑΩΡΟΝ ΚΑΙ ΣΥΝΕΛΗΦΘΗ ΕΙΣ ΜΟΝΑΧΟΝ

Ὑπὸ ἄκραν μυστικότητα καὶ σιωπὴν τῶν ἁρμοδίων ἀρχῶν ἀπεφυλακίσθη ὁ Γερμανὸς ἐγκληματίας πολέμου Μὰξ Μέρτεν χθὲς τὴν πρωίαν ἀπὸ τὰς φυλακὰς Ἀβέρωφ καὶ ἀνεχώρησεν εἰς Γερμανίαν, δι' ἀεροπλάνου τῆς Λουφτχάνσα.

Ἐνῶ ὅλαι αἱ ἁρμόδιαι ἀστυνομικαὶ ἀρχαί, ἡ διεύθυνσις τῶν φυλακῶν Ἀβέρωφ καὶ ἡ ἀεροπορικὴ ἑταιρία Λουφτχάνσα ἠρνοῦντο τὴν παροχὴν καὶ τῆς ἐλαχίστης ἔστω διαφωτιστικῆς πληροφορίας περὶ τῆς ὥρας καὶ τοῦ τρόπου τῆς ἀποφυλακίσεως καὶ

Ὁ πρῖγκιψ Ὀρσίνι πατὴρ τοῦ τέκνου

ΕΛΕΥΘΕΡΑ

ΔΥΣΚΟΛΟΝ εἶναι νὰ ἐννοήσῃ κανεὶς τί εἴδους εὐθιξία κατέλαβεν αἰφνιδίως τὰ μέλη τῆς Ἐπιτροπῆς διερευνήσεως ἀεροπορικῶν ἀτυχημάτων, ὥστε νὰ παραιτηθοῦν ὁμαδικῶς, ἐπειδὴ ἡ δικαστικὴ ἀρχὴ ἡ διεξάγουσα αὐτεπαγγέλτως ἀνάκρισιν ἐπὶ τοῦ δυστυχήματος τῆς «Ὀλυμπιακῆς Ἀεροπορίας» ὥρισε πραγματογνώμονας πρὸς ὑποβοήθησιν τοῦ ἔργου της. Ἡ μὲν Ἐπιτροπὴ διερευνήσεως εἶναι διοικητικὸν ὄρ-

ΑΝΑΓΚΑΣΤΙΚΗ ΠΡΟΣΓΕΙΩΣΙΣ ΤΟΥ ΕΠΗΝΔΡΩΜΕΝΟΥ ΑΜΕΡΙΚΑΝΙΚΟΥ ΠΥΡΑΥΛΟΥ

ΣΥΝΕΠΕΙΑ ΒΛΑΒΗΣ ΕΙΣ ΕΝΑ ΕΚ ΤΩΝ ΚΙΝΗΤΗΡΩΝ ΤΟΥ

ΑΕΡΟΠΟΡΙΚΗ ΒΑΣΙΣ ΕΝΤΟΥΑΡΝΤΣ, 5. (Ρώυτερ). — Τὸ πειραματικὸν ἀεροπλάνον-πύραυλος «Χ-15» μὲ χειριστὴν τὸν παλαίμαχον πιλότον Δοκίμων Σκὸτ Κρόσφηλντ, ὁ ὁποῖος πρόκειται νὰ ταξιδεύσῃ εἰς τὸ Διάστημα, ἐνήργησε σήμερον ἀναγκαστικὴν προσγείωσιν, ἀφοῦ προηγουμένως ἐξεκένωσε τὰ καύσιμά του.

Ὡς ἐδήλωσεν ὁ Κρόσφηλντ, ὀλίγον μετὰ τὸν ἀποχωρισμὸν τοῦ «Χ-15» ἀπὸ τοῦ βομβαρδιστικοῦ-φορέως τοῦ τύπου «Β-52» καὶ εὐθὺς ὡς εἶχον τεθῆ εἰς λει-

Fig. 28 Headline: Merten yesterday left for Germany

MERTEN IN THE POSTWAR YEARS

The First Years after the War

Until the end of 1946 Merten was a prisoner of war of the Americans and then a civilian internee in Dachau because of his administrative activity in Greece.[1] In August 1946 the Americans offered him to the Greeks as a potential war criminal but the responsible Greek commissioner, General Thomas Ypsilantis did not show any interest; but quite the contrary he pleaded for a quick release because Merten had behaved blamelessly in Saloniki.[2]

After his release from Dachau Merten approached the Greek military mission under Ypsilantis and offered to inform the Greek Government about his activities in Northern Greece during the war. The war crimes office (Grafeio Enklimaton Polemou) in Athens appreciated this, and on 13 January 1947 proposed that Merten should give testimony to the Greek military mission in Berlin. But this meeting did not take place.[3] Merten was not on any allied list of war criminals and in September 1948 the de-nazification (Entnazifizierung) tribunal put him in the category unburdened (unbelastet). Ypsilantis had assured the tribunal *"that Grece would no bring forward any charge against him [Merten]. In the opposite, we received reports about his good behaviour. If necessary we can obtain closer news about him from Greece."*[4]

Thus it can be stated here that no Greek Government raised any accusations against Merten immediately after the war. However the "National Office for War Crimes" had Merten on its wanted list since 1946.[5] But this did not mean much. Fleischer accurately described the status of this list: *"The lists contain numerous double mentions, frequent names (Müller etc.) or only first names without further evidence. Other persecuted are mentioned only identified with*

---

1 Wolfgang Breyer, *Dr. Max Merten - ein Militärbeamter der deutschen Wehrmacht im Spannungsfeld zwischen Legende und Wahrheit*, Diss. (Mannheim, 2003), p. 12f; Testimony of Merten to Amtsgericht Tiergarten Abt. 353 AR1680/61 on 29 Mai 1961.

2 "Griechenland Beziehungen. Die Falle der Fahndung" *Der Spiegel* 21 (22. Mai 1957), p. 15; Samuel Hassid, "The Trial of Max Merten in the Changing Mirros of Time and Place", in: http://greece.haifa.ac.il/events/holocaust_greece/Samuel_Hassid.pdf; Susanne-Sophia Spiliotis, *Der Fall Merten, Athen 1959: Ein Kriegsverbrecherprozeß im Spannungsfeld von Wiedergutmachungs- und Wirtschaftspolitik* MA-Thesis (München, 1991), p. 58f.

3 Spiliotis, *op. cit.*, p. 57f.

4 *"dass keine Klage von Seiten Griechenlands ... gegen ihn (Merten) erhoben wurde. Im Gegenteil, es sind uns Berichte über sein gutes Verhalten zugegangen. Falls erforderlich, können wir aus Griechenland nähere Nachrichten über ihn einholen."* Breyer, *op. cit.*, p. 13, p. 59 footnote 170.

5 Spiliotis, *op. cit.*, p. 59 footnote 170.

their miliary rank ('Feldwebel') or with garbled names (e.g. Rawglssf). Besides that all members of the mission and the general officers known by their names are mentioned often without any concrete criminal charge. He same is true for a part of the lists which the Greek state handed over to the German embassy in 1965."[1] Therefore it is not at all astonishing that Merten got onto that list.

On 6 January 1948 the "National Office for War Crimes" asked the Greek Foreign Ministry to file a motion with the Americans in Germany that Merten should be extradited because he was a war criminal. The motion was rejected because of formal mistakes. Besides that the motion came too late because since 1 November 1947 the list had been closed.[2] The real reason for the rejection originated from a totally different issue. In May 1947 General Bruno Bräuer had been executed in Athens without the slightest justification. He had been commander inn Crete and had done his best to stop reprisals. The Western Allies were so deeply shocked by this execution that from then on they did not any longer surrender any "war criminal" to Greece.[3] In 1948 a preliminary investigation by public prosecution ended with the accusation that Merten had been responsible for thc drafting of the Jews for forced labour and the arresting of several people.

1 *"Die Listen enthalten zahlreiche Doppelnennungen, Dutzendnamen (Müller etc.) oder auch nur Vornamen ohne weitere Angaben. Andere Gesuchte werden lediglich mit Dienstrang ('Feldwebel') oder mit verstümmeltem Namen (z. B: Rawglssf) 'identifiziert'. Darüber hinaus sind etwa alle namentlich bekannt gewordenen Mitglieder der Gesandtschaft und der Generalität pauschal erfaßt, oft ohne jeglichen konkreten Tatvorwurf. Die gleichen Einwände gelten für die z. T . identischen Listen, die der griechische Staat 1965 der deutschen Botschaft übergibt."* Hagen Fleischer, "Der Neubeginn in den Deutsch-Griechischen Beziehungen nach dem Zweiten Weltkrieg und die 'Bewältigung' der jüngsten Vergangenheit", in: Institute of Balkan Studies (ed.), *Griechenland und die Bundesrepublik Deutschland im Rahmen Nachkriegseuropas* (Thessaloniki: IMXA, 1989), p. 101 footnote 72; The list is printed in *Istorikon Archeion Ethnikis Antistaseos* 25-26 (September-October 1960), pp. 68-89. Merten appears twice; as Mertin Max Λοχαγός (Hauptmann - captain) and as Μέρτεν Μαξ Θεσσαλονίκη Στρατιωτικός (Militär). On the list were also the Generals Hellmut Felmy, Hubert Lanz and Wilhelm Speidel, which had been sentenced in the Nuremberg Trial and had been amnestied by McCloy, and the not amnestied General Wilhelm List, who was released from Landsberg because he was seriously ill. Additionally General Heinrich Kreipe was on list who on 1 March 1944 had taken over the command of the 22nd infantry division in Crete and had been kidnapped eight weeks later.

2 Spiliotis, *op. cit.*, p, 58.

3 Gerhard Weber, "Zu den Generalsprozessen. Unterschiede der Verfahren und Urteile über deutsche Besatzungsgeneräle in Griechenland" *Thetis* 18 (2011), p. 267.

According to the files of the Berlin Public Prosecutor in 1950 Merten allegedly applied for the position of German General Consul in Athens,[1] which is not very plausible because Merten had never been in the diplomatic service and in 1950 he opened a lawyer's office. However, if he really applied it is a kind of proof that he had no bad conscience. In 1952 Merten worked in the Ministry of Justice for some time but then he returned to his work as a lawyer. Politically Merten engaged himself in the *Gesamtdeutsche Volkspartei* of Gustav Heinemann which propagated a neutral united demilitarised Germany. This party was the most democratic one in the new FRG. Only convinced democrats joined it. This, however, did not hinder its opponents to denounce it as crypto-communist and have it supervised by the BND (Secret Service).

Earlier the Greek Government informed the German Embassy and Bonn that from 31 March 1957 on the arrest of war criminals would be resumed. Apparently this was not taken seriously and Merten was not warned.[2]

On 22 April 1957 Merten flew to Athens to do a business job of a client. Besides that he intended to bear witness in a private legal case of his former chief interpreter Arthur Meißner.[3] He passed the passport control without any problem. In order to be on the safe side that nothing would happen if he appeared in court on 23 April Merten went to the German Embassy and spoke to the head of the legal department, Ulrich Scheske, The latter told him that his appearance in court would be totally hazard-free. Thus reassured on 26 April Merten went to the court to give testimony. When he had finished it the judge had him arrested.[4]

In order to understand this we must have a look at the historical background which led to this development.

Greece's Financial Problems

Never since Greece became an independent state in 1832 had its budget been balanced; there had always been a gap which was closed by the protective power. From the 1860s on to 1947 this had been Great Britain. Then, in the

---

1 Hagen Fleischer, "Der Neubeginn in den Deutsch-Griechischen Beziehungen nach dem Zweiten Weltkrieg und die 'Bewältigung' der Jüngsten Vergangenheit," in: Institute of Balkan Studies (ed.), *Griechenland und die Bundesrepublik Deutschland im Rahmen Nachkriegseuropas* (Thessaloniki: IMXA, 1989), p. 97(

2 Görtemaker & Safferling, *op. cit.*, p. 324

3 Meißner had lived in Athens before the war and had worked as an interpreter during the occupation. After the surrender1945 his property a (a printer's shop) had been confiscated. In the actual trial it should decided whether the confiscation had been justified. "Griechenland Beziehungen. Die Falle der Fahndung" *Der Spiegel* 21 822. (Mai 1957), p. 16.

4 *Ibidem*, p. 56f.

context of the Truman Doctrine the US took over. But already in 1945 Greece tried to get a 250 million Dollar credit from the American Export-Import Bank. Not even a solvent borrower could have received such a sum. But the bank was ready to support a concrete program of Greece with 25 million Dollars. The State Department informed Ambassador MacVeagh accordingly. However first of all the talk about a 250 million credit should be stopped. MacVeagh informed the Greeks, but in Athens they continued to believe that the 250 million credit would be given and the 25 million were the first instalment. An official denial of the US Embassy did not have any effect.

MacVeagh angrily reported to Washington: *"It is most unfortunate that the question of the credit from the Export-Import Bank has been handled by the Greek Government in a manner which can only be described as careless. Greece needs almost everything that can be obtained from abroad, but there is little evidence of any sense of responsibility in arriving at a proper balance of requirements within reasonable limits of cost. Many of the requests submitted to UNRRA are frankly extravagant and the Eximbank list may well contain items of the same character."*[1]

The Greek Government showed a similar irresponsible attitude regarding the payment of reparations from Germany. In August the State Department had asked the Greek Government to prepare a list with their demands until October. On 17 October 1945 Symeon Diamantopoulos, the Greek ambassador in Washington presented the Greek demands. They amounted to the fantastic sum of 10,449,506,903 Dollars, a number which the American Ambassador characterised as "problematic",[2] when he mentioned it to Foreign Secretary Dean Acheson. At the same time the ambassador explained that the Greek government expected that foreign states would finance the reconstruction of the country. Apparently Greece relied on foreign help. In Washington the government was aghast at Greece's airy treatment of numbers.

First German Reparations

In February 1945 Roosevelt, Churchill and Stalin decided that Germany should pay for the damages it had caused as far as possible. However, Germany was totally destroyed and its economy was in a sorry state it was clear that Germany could not make any financial amends. Therefore material and

---

1 United States, Department of State, *Foreign Relations of the United States 1945,* VIII (Washington: Government Printing Office, 1969), p. 244. Quoted as FRUS.

2 *Ibidem*. The peace treaties concluded on the Paris peace conference in 1947 provided that Italy would pay 105 million Dollars and Bulgaria 50 million Dollars to Greece. Hungary should pay 200 millions and Rumania 300 million Dollars to the Soviet Union.

monetary values in Germany and from German assets held abroad should be confiscated. Goods of German production should be taken away annually. German labour could be used for reconstruction. All this should be controlled by an Allied Reparations Commission. In the Potsdam Conference the areas in Germany were defined from which the reparation goods were to be taken: The Western Powers and the countries, entitled to receive reparations, were to receive their goods from Western Germany, the Soviet Union and Poland primarily from Eastern Germany.

In the Paris Reparations Agreement of 14 February 1946 it was decided that the Western reparations demand should be divided among all states entitled to receive reparations with the exception of Poland and the Soviet Union. The conference conceded to Greece 4,5 percent of the material reparations and 2,7 percent of other reparations. The money assets which were to be distributed were the foreign assets of Germany and the so-called dismantling goods, which included everything that could be disassembled. All these decisions were authorized only by the Allies. The German side did not have any say, which is not astonishing since Germany was a state under occupation without an own government.[1] Later the distributed financial assets were estimated to have been 520 million Dollars market value of 1938. The value of the disassembled industrial plants was estimated lower. A final definition of the reparations question came on 27 February 1953 by the London Debt Agreement.[2]

During the post-war years big salvaging of industrial plants and other facilities e.g. hospitals took place in Western Germany which were transported to France and Britain as advance reparations. In 1948 Greece sent a commission to Western Germany which was to enforce the Greek demands. The material conceded to Greece consisted of *"30,000 tons machinery among it several train mills, a great number of machine tools, parts of cranes, facilities of casting houses and colour factories."* In 1948 the entire material was transported from the Ruhr area to Hamburg and there it was stored on dumb barges because no halls were available due to the bombing during the war.

In 1949 the material which had begun to corrode was put into a hall of MAN. In 1950 the first 10,000 tons were loaded on a British freighter and sent to Piraeus but it never arrived there. The remaining 18,500 tons went on corroding and blocked the MAN hall. In 1953 it became clear that the entire material had become worthless; it could only be scraped.

---

1 To come to the conclusion that these dismantled goods were no German reparations because the German government was not engaged is totally absurd.

2 Helmut Rumpf, "Die deutsche Frage und die Reparationen" *http://www.zaoerv.de* (1973).

The Greek commissioner responsible for the reparations was a certain Georgios Lavdas who remained in Bonn when the other commissioners left Germany. As *Der Spiegel* wrote Lavdas was mixed up in dark business dealings in which other members of the embassy also participated. Lavdas spent money like water. It had been he who had arranged that the first transport went on an English freighter and now he arranged that the scrap was sold to a British company though a German and an Italian company which offered better prices. It can be assumed that he earned a lot in both cases. What happened to the goods on the ships is unknown. Similarly it is unknown who got the money from the sale of the scrap.

However, it became a scandal when the journalist, Vasos Mathiopoulos, of the Plastiras newspaper *Allagi* wrote about it. In the Greek embassy in Bonn he was allegedly threatened with a good bashing if did not keep his mouth shut.[1] The value of the industrial goods was at least 30 million Dollars before they corroded, i.e 120 million DM at that time.

These industrial goods were excellent machines and production facilities which had been a part of the German armaments industry. In Britain these machincs ran til the late 1950s as I saw with my own eyes. If these machines and production facilities had reached Greece they certainly could have formed the nucleus of a manufacturing industry. The only beneficiary was apart of the Greek oligarchy which managed to acquire the revenues of the disappeared goods.

The 1952 London Debt Agreement

In 1949 the Federal Republic of Germany (FRG) came into being. In early 1950 the Cold War reached a first climax when the Korean war broke out. The Americans wanted that the FRG should rearm itself in order to strengthen the defence of Western Europe. Adenauer declared himself ready to do this but pointed out that either the FRG could rearm or pay reparations. To do both would outrun the economic power of the FRG. The Americans, however, wanted the rearmament. Now long difficult negotiations began which ended 1953 with the London Debt Agreement.

In the London Debt Agreement of 27 February 1953 it was decided that German reparations would be paid only when the two Germanies were reunited or by bi-lateral agreements. Since in 1953 nobody could imagine that the two inimical Germanies would ever be reunited the reparations were post-

1 "Reparationen. Dein Maul zu halten" *Der Spiegel* (22. Oktober 1952).

poned until doomsday. Greece and Yugoslavia also signed this agreement.[1] With this agreement the FRG had a legal basis to reject all demands for reparations before the re-unification of Germany.

But there were two exceptional cases: Yugoslavia and Greece. When Nikita Khrushchev visited Yugoslavia in the mid-1950s the US became afraid that Yugoslavia might drift again to the Eastern Block. In order to prevent this the US pressed Bonn to pay reparations to Yugoslavia. Bonn did this and paid 60 million DM cash to Yugoslavia and an investment credit of 240 million DM with a credit period of 99 years.

Greek Efforts to Get German Financial Aid

Since the Truman Doctrine of 1947 the Greek politicians relied on the Americans that they would fill the Greek budget gap and would support Greece financially. McNeill described this behaviour accurately: *"Greek politicians found no real need to do more than agree in words with American demands for economy and reorganization in government. So long as the Americans were prepared to pump hundreds of millions of dollars into the economy each year, why should the Greek government not run an unbalanced budget and let the balance of foreign payments take care of itself? The Americans would have to make the deficits good; and if they complained of the use to which their funds were put, one would mollify them with promises for the future. [...] The United States owed them a great debt of gratitude for having fought the guerilla war and stopped the advance of Communism. [...] Some politicians were even inclined to feel that it would not really be a good thing to balance the budget and correct the shortfall in exports, for if these things were done, then the crying need for American aid would disappear, and the country might then be left to fend for itself economically."*[2]

However in 1953 the Republican Eisenhower administration chose to finish closing the chronic gap in the Greek budget and drastically curtailed the supporting payments. The American behaviour made it clear to the Greeks that from now on they could not expect substantial economic aid. In Athens it was understood that one needed other money sources and Britain and the FRG were the first candidates. In July 1953 Markezinis visited London and had talks with governmental authorities and outstanding business leaders which all

1 Christoph Buchheim, "Das Londoner Schuldenabkommen", in: Ludolf Herbst (ed.): *Westdeutschland 1945–1955. Unterwerfung, Kontrolle, Integration* (München; Oldenbourg, 1986),pp. 219–229.

2 William Hardy McNeill, *Greece: American Aid in Action 1947-1956* (New York: The Twentieth Century Fund, 1957), p. 61.

were very cordial but brought no results.[1] Therefore the FRG remained the only candidate.

In 1953 Markezinis visited Bonn and after his return he announced that the German Government had promised to grant a credit of 200 million DM. Because Adenauer intended to visit Greece in March 1954 a credit garantor had to be found. Though the minister of finance rejected the credit the cabinet decided to authorize the *Kreditanstalt für Wiederaufbau* (credit bank for reconstruction) to give a tax privileged credit of 250 million DM.[2] Thus an unstressed visit of Adenauer in Athens on 9 March was assured.

Adenauer's visit in Greece was the first visit of a German head of government. The official program lasted from 10 to 12 March 1954. Adenauer made some conciliatory gestures and his daughter handed over a cheque of 50,000 DM to Queen Frederica for the reconstruction of Kalavryta. This gesture, however, was made in vain because the Queen misplaced the cheque and found it again after eight months.[3] Whether the money arrived in Kalavryta is unknown However Adenauer's voyage to Greece fullfilled with substance the agreement about economic cooperation. From then on German industry was expected to contribute to the reconstruction of Greece and promote the country economically by investments. The Greek side promised to restore former property of the German Reich to the FRG.[4]

In June 1954 Prime Minister Papagos appeared in Bonn for a return visit. He brought with him a bill which had passed the Greek parliament just before his visit. It dealt with the restitution of former German financial assets. An agreement on economic questions was signed. In November 1954 Ludwig Erhard, Minister of economic, visited Athens. The German financial assets were restored and Erhard prolonged the term of the credit substantially and agreed that the import quantity of Greek wines and tobacco should be increased. One had arrived at the *quid pro quo* system i.e. in normalcy.[5]

---

1 Spyros Linardatos, *Apo ton emfylio sti chounta,* II (Athen: Papazisis, 1977), p. 89f.

2 22nd session of the Cabinet on 8 March 1954 C. "Finanzierung Industrieller Vorhaben in Griechenland". http://www.bundesarchiv.de/cocoon/barch/0000/k/k1954k/kap1_2/-kap2_9/para3_5.html

3 Ehrengard Schramm, *Ein Hilfswerk für Griechenland. Begegnungen und Erfahrungen mit Hinterbliebenen deutscher Gewalttaten der Jahre 1941-1944* (Göttingen: Vandenhoeck & Ruprecht, 2003), p. 53.

4 Olga Lazaridou, *Von der Krise zur Normalität, Die deutsch-griechischen Beziehungen unter besonderer Berücksichtigung der politischen und wirtschaftlichen Grundlagen (1949-1958)* Diss. (Bonn, 1992), p. 165.

5 Lazaridou, *op. cit.*, p. 179f.

In 1955 Karamanlis became Prime Minister. Like his predecessors he tried to get American economic aid. But by the Eisenhower doctrine only directly threatened states received aid. During talks in Washington he reminded the relevant people that the US had always paid the deficit in the Greek budget. The Americans reacted friendly but remained noncommittal.[1] Thus it was clear that Karamanlis had to find other money sources. He did not want credits which would increase the debt of the country but payments which would not have to be repaid. However with the exception of the US no other state could grant such lost benefits, let alone then the FRG.

The German-Yugoslav negotiation had been watched in Athens and when the results became known in October 1956 Athens in the person of trade minister Panagiotis Papaligouras addressed the German Embassy in Athens demanding economic aid. The minister mentioned the help which Yugoslavia had obtained. The FRG was the most important trade partner of Greece and the strongest economic force in Europe. Economic aid would keep Greece in the Western camp. Papaligouras casually hinted that Germany had the duty to pay reparations to Greece for the war damages. The Greek Government was thinking of a long term credit.[2] Thus the Greek side tried to imitate the Yugoslav proceeding and obtain reparations camouflaged as a long term credit.

The German Ambassador Theo Kordt recommended a benevolent examination of the Greek wish. The AA was against a rejection of the wish but the Ministry of Finance rejected it as before in the Yugoslav case. There were no means for credits to foreign states. Another precedent should not be created. Besides that, the budgetary position of the FRG was strained. The Ministry of Economics saw the case in a more differentiated manner. Greece had suffered more from WWII and the civil war than Yugoslavia. The Greek press attacked the Athens government because it did not demand reparations from the FRG as Yugoslavia had done. Since the Eastern Block tried to penetrate the Greek market by offering cheap goods, it would be reasonable to help the Greeks with 150-200 million DM credit and a minimum term of 10-20 years. The necessary means for this could be taken out of the budget of the developmental aid.[3]

In early March ambassador Kordt reported that the demands for reparations were vehemently discussed in the Greek parliament and the demand for German economic aid became stronger. The question of the reparations, which had not been paid, was suitable to make the feelings run high, precisely be-

---

1 *FRUS 1955-1957*, XXIV, pp. 574-576.

2 Lazaridou, *op. cit.*, p. 211f.

3 *Ibidem*, p. 213f.

cause Greece had signed the London Debt Agreement this increased the moral pressure on Germany to grant Greece extensive economic aid.[1] When in March 1957 vice-chancellor Franz Blücher visited Athens and met Karamanlis the latter spoke about the economic help. In April and May these talks continued and the Yugoslav aid was mentioned. During the Greek-German economic discussions at the end of May Economic Minister Erhard gave to understand that Germany was principally ready to assist the Greek economic reconstruction by granting so-called Hermes monetary bonds but the granting of government bonds would be a total political *novum*. The Yugoslav bonds had been granted out of political reasons and for such topics the Foreign Minister was the correct contact person. By this statement Erhard signalled that he advocated support for Greece.[2]

At the beginning of June the process of forming an opinion among the various departments of the German government was roughly finished. It was agreed that Greece should be helped. The grant of a bond, however, was excluded because such a bond needed the agreement of the parliament which would be difficult to obtain because elections were imminent. However the financing of long term investments should be checked. The Greek side, however, insisted and mentioned the unpaid reparations for war destructions in order to put pressure on the process. In early July Bonn decided that Greece would receive a low coupon credit of 50-75 million DM.[3] Whether this change of opinion had been caused by the Greek demand of reparations is unclear but it might have played a role.

From 6 to 10 July 1957 minister of trade Papaligouras came to Bonn invited by vice-chancellor Blücher. During these talks the Greek deliveries of ammunition to Germany were one topic. Papaligouras on the other hand informed his partners in Bonn about Greek plans of developing the infra- structure. Because of supply difficulties of the Greeks and changes of the armament of the German army (Bundeswehr) the ammunitions project could be implemented only in a rather restricted form. Undersecretary of state, Westrick, of the Ministry of Economics suggested to support the electrical power plant of Ptolemaida in the lignite area by a German credit. Adenauer considered this project as the only feasible one.[4]

---

1 *Ibidem*, p. 215f.
2 *Ibidem*, p. 217f.
3 *Ibidem*, p. 218f.
4 *Ibidem*, p. 220f; 188. Cabinet session on 10 July 1957: http://www.bundesarchiv.de/cocoon/barch/0000/k/k1957k/kap1_2/kap2_29/para3_11.html: http://www.bundesarchiv.de/cocoon/barch/0000/k/k1958k/kap1_2/kap2_24/para3_12.html.

Papaligouras returned to Athens highly satisfied. Since Bonn, however, did nothing to keep the promise frustration in Athens was growing because it was noticed that Bonn accommodated the Yugoslavs. In November 1957 the economic talks were resumed but did not lead to any concrete result.

Negotiations about the Treatment of the War Criminals

Already in the 1950 during the economic negotiations between the Greek Vice-Premier Papandreou and the German Minister for Economic Affairs, Ludwig Erhard, the overcoming of the sinister past was a topic. Erhard demanded the restoration of confiscated German assets. When in 1951 negotiations for the resumption of diplomatic relations began it became clear that the settlement of the question of the the war criminals was a precondition. The McCloy amnesty of 1951 made this easier. In June 1951 diplomatic relations were restored. Already at the end of this month first arrangements were granted: Impeached war criminals now could raise an objection. The German side, however, urged for a quiet settlement. The Greek government was ready to transfer the so-called war criminals and the material of evidence to Germany which would put them on trial if they were guilty. Thus in the case of general Alexander Andrae, who in 1947 had been condemned to lifelong prison, the prison sentence was reduced to four years and in early 1952 he was secretly deported to the FRG. The Greek public learned about it and was outraged: This was a case of barter trade: Tobacco for a life.[1]

In the spring of 1952 the legal preconditions were made to transfer the prosecution to the German side. In August the deputy General State Prosecutor and chief of war criminal office, Andreas Tousis, appeared in Bonn. He transferred the first 22 class-action lawsuits against roughly 200 defendants to the German judiciary. The remaining easier cases would be struck down by the passing of a special law. Tousis said the if the German justice would press charges against the 22 main cases the Greek criminal proceedings would be suspended. The Greek minister of justice considered this as a contribution to the internal pacification of Greece and the restoration of good relations with Germany.[2]

It was obvious that the Greek coalition governments under Plastiras and Venizelos tried to meddle with the judiciary for political reasons in order to obtain the benevolence of the FRG government in economic matters. Thus they created a precedent to which the Karamanlis Government returned in

1 "Griechenland Beziehungen. Die Falle der Fahndung" *Der Spiegel* 21 (22 Mai 1957), pp. 5-8

2 *Ibidem*, pp. 12-15.

1959. The German judiciary on the other side treated the cases transferred by the Greeks in such a dilatory way that the Greek war criminal office asked in a most courteous way what had been done in the 22 cases. The German reply took time. For domestic political reasons the Greeks now suggested that the final 100-150 lawsuits should be transferred to the German judiciary and not, as originally planned, dismissed. Only the last 150 easy cases would be taken care of by an amnesty.[1]

The forthcoming sovereignty of the FRG in 1955 strengthened the tendency to do even less in the question of the sentencing of the war criminals. It was hoped that one could wipe the slate clean, without trials of the war criminals and the remnants of national socialist past. A general amnesty was considered but as such a law could have provoked political damage alternatives were search for. It was assumed that Athens also would be ready to finish all lawsuits inconspicuously. Therefore in summer 1955 the FRG declared itself ready *"to accept all pending actions in Greece provided the Greek government considers the matter as finished with the handing over and the transfer and does not insist an information of the further treatment in the FRG."*[2]

Thus, all cases of the past and the still pending ones would have been finished at one stroke. There was no desire to clear the war crimes committed in Greece and bring them to court. The vivid correspondence between the AA and the embassy in Athens proves that a way was sought how to solve this problem as silently as possible. The BMJ and the AA would have preferred an unofficial verbal agreement without a written document.[3] However, this or an general amnesty would have caused trouble in Greece and for the new Karamanlis government even to considered it. Therefore, all criminal proceedings should be transferred to the German federal government and Greece should relinquish the right of the Greek state to impose punishment.

Finally in April 1956 negotiations began which lasted til June. Tousis was ready to transfer all cases to the BMJ and suspend them: He expected, on the other hand, that the German judiciary become active. The German side, however, expected a Greek agreement that would accept German inactivity. Since Tousis did not massively object the German side believed that Tousis

---

1 *Ibidem*, p. 21.

2 *"alle in Griechenland anhängigen Verfahren entgegenzunehmen, vorausgesetzt, dass die griechische Regierung die Angelegenheit mit der Übernahme und Abgabe der Vorgänge als erledigt ansieht und nicht auf Auskunft über ihre weitere Behandlung in der Bundesrepublik besteht."* AA an Botschaft Athen am 22. Juli 1955 BA/ZWA 3 141/9564. P. 17, quoted by Spiliotis, *op. cit.*, p. 24.

3 *Ibidem*, p. 25.

accepted its opinion. It was not understood that Tousis wanted to implement his own judicial conceptions which were not identical with that of the Greek government. The final protocol of 7 June 1956 shows clearly that Tousis agreed to a suspension in Greece only if the German judiciary became active. The German side promised this but gave to understand that this would take quite a lot of time due to technical reasons. Obviously the German side intended to continue its policy of doing nothing. The Bonn cabinet had the impression that the question of the war criminals was finished.[1] However, this was a deceptive conclusion as would be soon seen.

Tousis understood that he was returning to Greece with empty hands. The Greek side had made concessions but had received nothing in turn. The principle of do ut des had been disregarded. However, exactly at this time the negotiations of trade minister Panagiotis Papaligouras began in Bonn about economic aid which in reality were reparations in disguise. Besides that in June 1956 Greece and several other European states had addressed a note to the Bonn government demanding compensation for the victims of NS persecutions. Tousis had the idea to link the release of an amnesty with these demands to quieten the Greek public. It is not clear which of the two demands was meant at this point. As we will show this was changed every now and then according to opportunity. The Greek foreign ministry took over this idea and on 27 November 1956 addressed a memorandum to the German Embassy which said that an amnesty for all war criminals would be released if the FRG was ready to pay compensations to the victims of the war. Thus a linkage between amnesty and reparations was created.

At the same time governmental talks began about the termination of the judicial assessment of the crimes committed during the occupation. On 27 November 1956 the Greek Foreign Ministry submitted a memorandum to the German Embassy which stated that an amnesty would be released for all war criminals if the Federal Republic was ready to pay compensations to all war casualties. Thus a junctim had been created between an amnesty and reparations.[2] The AA (Foreign Ministry) and the Federal Ministry of Justice (BMJ) regarded this Greek proposal as another attempt to undermine the London Debt Agreement and therefore rejected it. One should try to avoid the im-

---

1 *"dass die Bundesregierung vielleicht bereit sein würde, nach Einstellung der in Griechenland anhängigen Strafverfahren, über die Frage einer Entschädigung mit sich reden zu lassen." Ibidem*, pp. 28- 34.

2 Spiliotis, *op. cit.*, pp. 40-45.

pression, *"that the federal government might be ready, after the abeyance of the cases pending in Greece, to talk about the question of reparations."*[1]

Public prosecutor, Andreas Tousis, urged the German Embassy that Bonn should make a gesture then could be the prosecution measurements suspended. Ambassador Kordt warned Bonn in early April: The only way out of the impasse would be the acceptance of the Greek proposal for reparations and to signal readiness for negotiations: *"The release of an amnesty law, which could make a final stroke under this heritage of the past, will be impossible without a regulation of the reparations question of the victims of the crimes."* Unfortunately Kordt's word did not encounter open ears in Bonn and the AA did not react. On 23 April the Federal Ministry of Justice (BMJ) rejected any reparation payments categorically and regarded the Greek threat to start again the persecution measures as not justified. as was stated before.[2] Obviously nobody in Bonn could imagine that the Greeks would act. But one day before the German citizen Max Merten who was on the persecution list had arrived in Athens.

Without Merten's arrival in Athens Tousis threats would have been idle because there were no German war criminals in Greece who might have been arrested. Merten's arrival in Athens, however, changed everything. It can be assumed that Merten's readiness to give testimony in the Meißner trial became known to the Greek judiciary and it had been announced to the War Crime Office. And Merten's name was on that list. It was a perfect timing. On the other hand it must be stated here that the arrest of Merten was accidental. Had another person whose name was on the list entered Greece he would have been arrested. The assumption that Merten was arrested because, with him as a kind of hostage, the demand for reparations from the Bonn government would be successful due to Merten's political weight is a wrong interpretation. In 1957 Merten was a simple lawyer and citizen.

---

1 *Ibidem*, pp. 46-49.

2 *"Die Einbringung eines Amnestiegesetzes, das allein einen Schlußstrich unter dieses Erbe der Vergangenheit setzen kann, wird aber ohne Regelung der Entschädigungsfrage für die Opfer der Straftaten nicht möglich sein."* - *Ibidem*, pp. 50-54.

German Reactions

The German Embassy rather quickly understood that the forthcoming trial against Merten was used to apply pressure in order to come to a solution of the reparations question. It was hoped that the whole affair would go off without a hitch.[1] On 15 May 1957 the Embassy informed the AA that the Greek Government had tried all tricks to get reparation money. On 29 April the AA instructed the Embassy to demand the immediate release of Merten and his unhindered departure. The position of the Federal Government in the reparations question was known.[2] On 16 May the Embassy reported to the AA that a suspension of the trial could only be achieved in connection with an arrangement of the reparations question. It was recommended that the AA should examine this benevolently

On 20 May counsellor of embassy in Athens, Gustav von Schmoller, reminded the AA that *"that Greece suffered a lot by Germany and had big losses of people and economic goods."* It should be understood that Greece expected a reward because they had been generous in question of the war criminals. Bonn should examine the Greek proposals quickly.[3]

On the same day the AA demanded that the Merten case should be totally separated from the reparations question. The Federal Ministry of Justice (BM-J) suggested to exert pressure on Greece in case Merten was not released. A representative of the AA suggested to issue travel warnings to all those who had been in Greece during WWII. Athens was angry because the Yugoslavs had received 320 million DM reparations. The economic situation of Greece was so disparate that Athens was ready to use every means to get money. The Embassy should be informed that Bonn would not accept any package deal.[4] On 23 May the AA instructed the embassy to demand the immediate release of Merten and his outward voyage. The position of the Federal Government regarding reparation was known.[5]

---

1 Spiliotis, op. cit. p. 64. BA/B 305-1041.

2 BA B 141/9566, p. 51.

3 *"Griechenland [...] durch deutsche Schuld schwer gelitten und im Krieg hohe Verluste an Menschen und Wirtschaftsgütern [hat] hinnehmen müssen."* Hagen Fleischer,& Despina Konstantinakou, „Ad calendas graecas? Griechenland und die deutsche Wiedergutmachung", in: Hans Günter Hockerts,, Claudia Moisel & Tobias Winstel, /eds.) *Grenzen der Wiedergutmachung: die Entschädigung für NS-Verfolgte in West- und Osteuropa,* (Göttingen, 2006), p. 400.

4 Aktenvermerk des DBMdJ 9250/1-3-12562/57 vom 20. Mai 1957. BA B 141/9566, pp. 37-44.

5 BA B 141/9566, p. 51.

As the Embassy knew that the behaviour of the Greeks was attributed to the German inactivity in the question of the war criminals it reacted reluctantly. Instead of stating its "discontent", it expressed its regret and asked for further suspension of the other proceedings. During a conversation of Scheske and Tousis it became clear that Tousis intended to go the whole hog judicially and was not ready to show any political respect. The Embassy told the AA that it would continue trying to get a suspension of the other cases but if it did not succeed in doing this, the best would be to issue a travel warning. A suspension of the case could only be achieved by a regulation of the reparations question. The Embassy recommended that the AA should examine this benevolently.[1]

On 22 May Der Spiegel wrote: *"The answer to this enigma is that Merten became the first victim of a dispute during which the Greek government has been trying by well known Balkan methods for one year to put pressure to the Federal Government and make it pay unscheduled reparations."*[2] This article and some similar ones in German newspapers triggered prosecutor Tousis to angry reactions as is shown by an Embassy report of 3 June: *"The way how this topic is treated appears strange to him, especially he felt hurt by the accusation of Balkan methods of the Greek Government."* The German Government should do the same as he had done when he forbade the Greek press to write about the preliminary investigations against Merten. The Embassy told Tousis that the German Government had no means to stop the press report as the Greek press law permitted. The AA was asked why the German press described Merten as a victim. The role of a martyr did not suit Merten.[3]

In March 1957 the Greek Ministry of Justice announced a list of the criminal acts which Merten had allegedly committed: Murder, internment of Greeks in the Pavlos-Melas-Prison, confiscation of Jewish fortunes, plundering of Jewish shops, compelling of Jews to forced labour and direct participation in the destruction of the the Jewish population. Merten's arrest and this report was of interest for the Athenian press. Schmoller, however, noticed that not all articles in the papers were anti-German. The Jewish bi-weekly, *Evraiki Estia,* pub-

---

1 RK 515-10 Ber. Nr. 533/57 vom 16. Mai 1957 BA B 141/9566, pp. 62-67.

2 *"Die Lösung des Rätsels ist, dass Merten das erste Opfer einer Auseinandersetzung wurde, in deren Verlauf die griechische Regierung seit einem Jahr auf gut balkanische Weise versucht, die Bundesregierung unter Druck zu setzen und sie zu außerplanmäßigen Reparationsleistungen zu veranlassen."*"Griechenland Beziehungen. Die Falle der Fahndung" *Der Spiegel* 21 (22. Mai 1957), p. 15.

3 *"Die Art der Behandlung des Themas befremde ihn, vor allem fühle er sich durch den Vorwurf der 'balkanischen Methoden der griechischen Regierung' getroffen."* RK 515-10 Ber. Nr. 598 (57 vom 3. Juni 1957 BA B 141/9566, pp. 80-81.

lished an appeal on its front-page to inform the investigating judge about crimes committed by Merten. The newspaper *To Vima* even wrote about the possibility of death penalty. When the German embassy protested the Greek government imposed a publication verdict in the Merten case.[1]

Ambassador Schmoller of the Athens Embassy repeatedly warned Bonn. But the AA and the BMJ remained in their negative attitude. The latter proved to be especially stubborn and arrogant when it demanded from the Greeks that they to suspend the impending case. Schmoller warned again: *"If the Greek proposal will be rejected by referring to the London Debt Agreement the the trails will executed with all afore mentioned annoying consequences and with no regard to straining German Greek relations."*[2] But Bonn remained stubborn. They believed that the Greeks only wanted money. This became obvious during the parallel economic negotiations.[3]

Then the BMJ tried a trick: The persecution of the war criminals, who had been in Greece, had been active in Germany and as proof of this the BMJ submitted a list of cases. But it was easy to recognize that this list had been prepared *ad hoc* because almost all cases carried the date 1957, i.e. the were new cases. Additionally, it did not show the numbers of the files. Schmoller came to the conclusion, that the Ministry of Justice was not interested in an investigation and punishment of teh accused. The Greeks had understood the transfer of the cases in 1952 and 1956 had only one purpose *"to impede the cases in Greece. [...] In my opinion we cannot put demands in this case. Germans committed crimes in Greece and the right of the state to inflict punishment is not prescribed nor is the recollection of the ordeals of occupation of the people erased. If the Greek Government submits a proposal for a solution of the problem I would be grateful if in the context of our general relations it should be examined and this especially as the Greek side*

---

1 *"den Fortgang der Verfahren in Griechenland zu hemmen.. [...] Meines Erachtens haben wir hier keine Forderungen zu stellen. Deutsche haben in Griechenland Straftaten begangen und der Strafanspruch des griechischen Staates ist ebensowenig verjährt wie die Erinnerung des Volkes an die Leiden der Besatzungszeit gelöscht ist. Wenn die griechische Regierung einen Vorschlag zur Lösung des Problems vorlegt, so wäre ich im Interesse unserer Gesamtbeziehungen dankbar, wenn er geprüft wird, zumal die griechische Seite in der bisherigen Behandlung der Verfahren im Rahmen des Gesetzes wirklich bis an die Grenze des Möglichen gegangen ist."* Katerina Kralowa, *Das Vermächtnis der Besatzung. Deutsch-griechische Beziehungen seit 1940* (Köln: Böhlau, 2016), p. 153f.

2 *"Wird der griechische Vorschlag unter Berufung auf das Londoner Schuldenabkommen a limine abgelehnt, so werden die Prozesse mit allen geschilderten unerfreulichen Folgen und ohne Rücksicht auf die Belastung des deutsch-griechischen Verhältnisses durchgeführt werden."* Spiliotis, *op. cit.*, p. 69.

3 *Ibidemt.*, p. 71.

went to the border of possibility in the context of the procedure in the framework of the law."[1]

Bonn, however, was not ready to give in. The AA looked for honest witnesses for the defence and developed a slightly abstruse ideas. The Siemens Company should be questioned about Dimitrios Makris who had been its local lawyer during the occupation and was now Minister of Justice.[2] However after the exchange of more messages between the Embassy in Athens and the AA in Bonn it became clear that Bonn had to move.

The first proposal showed that Bonn had not grasped the real matter. One was ready to start a trial against Merten in Germany. For this purpose Merten should be transferred to Germany for interrogation while Greece would tacitly accept that he would not return.[3] Obviously it was not understood in Bonn that such games were excluded in the meantime. Nevertheless AA and BMJ decided to send the former chief of the German delegation, Ernst Kanter, who had led the negotiations in 1952 and 1956 to Athens with the mission to find a solution. Kanter met Merten's lawyer Matsoukas and told him that the accusations against Merten were unfounded. As a former military judge Kanter knew the occupation system very well and that a *Kriegsverwaltungsrat* had not had the right to order executions, deportations or persecution of the Jews.[4]

On 25 July Kanter and Tousis met. Kanter "proved" that war criminals were punished in Germany. He even alleged that a procedure had been opened against Merten. But this procedure did not progress because Merten was in a Greek jail. Kanter proposed a extradition. Tousis rejected this because Merten had "committed his crimes" in Greece and was in court there. The court responsible for his case would reject any extradition. However, he and the Government were interested in a quick settlement without a trial. As soon as the preliminary investigation were concluded the press could no longer be restrained. *"Therefore it was advisable to clear the question soon (if necessary by rendition or transfer). The solution, however, is not a case of the judiciary but of the political authorities."* Tousis then spoke about reparations. Reparations would be the best possibility for a detente. *"It should not be considered as if the Greek Government made the case Merten a case for negotiations trying to knock out a ransom."* But the proposal should be

---

1 Schmoller an AA am 27. Mai 1957: BA/ZWA B 141/9566, p. 56, quoted from. Spiliotis, *op. cit.*, p. 75f.

2 Spiliotis, *op. cit.*, p. 77.

3 *Ibidem*, p. 83.

4 Manfred Görtemaker & Christoph Safferling, *Die Akte Rosenberg. Das Bundesministerium der Justiz und die NS-Zeit* (München: Beck, 2016), p. 315.

examined. *"By the way according to his opinion and the opinion of the competent government circles a small guaranty fonds would suffice. He just thought of a symbolic gratuity."*[1]

Several times Tousis assured that *"no blackmailing of a ransom was intended."* Kanter came to the conclusion that Germany had not behaved in the proper way in the past. *"We made it very difficult for Greece to treat us obligingly concerning the question of the war criminals. Despite several oral questions we did not tell them the state of affairs about them."* The initiated criminal proceedings in Germany should be expedited quickly, so the impression created in Greece of a "casual execution" could be avoided. The Greek side should be informed that they could end the parallel cases in Greece. Additionally a political solution should be sought.[2]

After a lot of to and fro on 17 October the German minister of justice, Hans-Joachim von Merkatz, resignedly stated in a letter to Foreign Minister von Brentano that the Merten case could not be solved by judicial means. The difficulties created by the Merten case could only be solved by Greek-German negotiations about reparations. One had to talk about reparations. Tousis had hinted that by such negotiation the Merten case could take a different development. Only that way something could be accomplished. Though this did not conform with the London Agreement it was the only way to overcome the Greek-German tensions.[3]

The AA however rejected the Greek demand for reparations. The Embassy should insist on the transfer of Merten or demand a speedy trial. The AA was afraid that the Greek Government would postpone the trial for of fear of a battle with the opposition in the press. Therefore Merten would remain in jail for a long time without any trial. At the same time the central legal protection

---

1 *"Daher sei es ratsam, die Frage der Bereinigung des Verfahrens (gegebenenfalls durch Auslieferung oder Überstellung) bald zu klären. Die Lösung sei aber keine Sache der Justiz, sondern der politischen Instanzen."* - *"Es dürfe nicht so aufgefasst werden, als ob die griechische Regierung den Fall Merten zu einem Handelsobjekt mache und etwa ein Lösegeld herausschlagen wolle."* - *"Im übrigen werde nach seiner Auffassung und auch nach Auffassung der zuständigen Regierungsstellen ein verhältnismäßig kleiner Garantiefonds genügen. Es sei lediglich an eine symbolische Abfindung gedacht."* Memo on the conversation with Tousis on 25 July 1947. BA B 141/9566, pp. 141-143.

2 *"nicht etwa eine Erpressung mit Lösegeld beabsichtigt sei."* - *"Wir haben es Griechenland sehr schwer gemacht, uns in der Kriegsverbrecherfrage entgegenkommend zu behandeln. Wir haben den Griechen trotz mehrfacher mündlicher Anfragen nicht mitgeteilt, wie es mit der Einleitung unserer Verfahren stehe."* Memo on Kanter's trip of 7 August 1957: BA B 141/9566, pp. 152-157.

3 Letter Merkatz to Brentano on 17 Oktober 1957: BA B 141/9566, pp. 204-206

department of the AA tried to find exonerating evidence for the defence of Merten.[1]

On 5 March 1958 the Karamanlis Government resigned. King Paul installed an interim government which was to prepare the elections on 11 May. On 15 March 1958 the Greek Government gave a memorandum to the German Embassy in which it again proposed reparations as a solution for the whole war criminal problem. Though the Greek Government knew that Germany rejected this, it assured it of further readiness for cooperation. Though the Government did not have any influence on the judiciary it promised an early act of grace if he were convicted. But the AA continued to try to free Merten without making any concession on the reparation question. The AA developed the idea that Federal President Heuss might appeal to King Paul. The Greek side also began to think about how to wind up the case in a quiet manner. But all this did not lead anywhere because at the end of March the chamber responsible for war criminal cases decided to transfer the Merten case to a special military court. This decision was taken because a military court could be controlled by the Government. Additionally a military court was not obliged to check the truth of the statements of witnesses for the defence, or of the prosecution.

With this decision the box of Pandora was opened because from now on the press and the left EDA party could participate. The Merten case became the vehicle of the opposition against the conservative Government of Karamanlis who had been reelected.. Because the atmosphere in Greece was heating any deportation was excluded. Because of the internal political mudslinging a transfer of Merten to Germany was impossible, even the death penalty was threatening Merten. Resigning Ambassador Kordt stated that one could not stop developments.[2] One can speculate whether without the weak interim Government Tousis would have dared to take this decisive step.

In Bonn the AA had brought itself to make a new offer to the Greeks. One would inform the Greek Government that the pre-trial proceedings against Merten would be speeded up and thus the main trial would soon occur. Thus an extradition of Merten would be possible for the Greek side. At the same time it would be signalled to the Greeks that, if they assured to transfer Merten sooner or later, an economic delegation could be sent to Bonn to talk about economic support. By this it became clear that Bonn accepted a link between the Merten case and the economic aid: *"The economic help wanted by the Greek side strengthens our position. The German embassy might cautiously*

---

1 Spiliotis, *op. cit.*, p. 96f.
2 *Ibidem*, pp. 98-101.

hint to the Greek Foreign Minister that the German public would not understand it if such negotiations began before the Merten case is solved."[1] These indications were made and a little later of a special law condoning war criminals was enacted. It was a signal towards Bonn. Obviously new talks were wanted to avoid further damage of the bilateral relations by the Merten case.

Tousis behaviour regarding the compensation of the Jewish Greeks was most astonishing. If the claims for damages of the Greeks were compensated a legal amnesty solution could include Merten. The enforcement of damage claims of the Jew Tousis considered futile. This attitude was not understood by the German side since the EDA made great fuss about this question. Most probably Tousis blocked this reparations demand because pressed for it by the Left. It is possible, however, that he assumed that reparation payment for Greece only could be obtained more easily because the Jewish demand comprised many western states and was much larger. But it should be noted here, that Tousis was only interested in pushing through the Greek demands.[2]

Since May 1958 the Greek manhunt machinery went full speed. In mid-June 1958 Schmoller, councillor of the German Embassy complained in the Greek Foreign Ministry that *"recently German citizens, who come to Greece as tourists or stay in Greece receive summons of the police or are persecuted by it, are suspected to have committed war crimes in Greece."* The report of the embassy added that Tousis was trying to build up additional pressure *"to make the German side more inclined towards his proposal to begin negotiation about the question of payment of reparations."* These measures were only directed against innocent people because criminal proceedings had been set in motion in Germany. These people were warned and would certainly not travel to Greece. If these persecutions went on a general travel warning should be issued.[3]

---

1 *"Die von griechischer Seite angestrebte deutsche Wirtshaftshilfe verstärkt unsere Position. Die deutsche Botschaft wird beim Außenminister in Griechenland vorsichtig durchblicken lassen, dass es in der deutschen Öffentlichkeit nicht verstanden würde, wenn solche Verhandlungen vor der Regelung des Falles Merten stattfänden."* AA (Ref. 503) - Memo of 22 May 1958: BA/B 305-1047. Quoted from. Spiliotis, *op. cit.*, p. 103.

2 Spiliotis, *op. cit.*, pp. 105-108.

3 *"in letzter Zeit immer wieder deutsche Staatsangehörige, die entweder als Touristen nach Griechenland kommen oder sich hier ständig aufhalten, unter dem Verdacht, in Griechenland Kriegsverbrechen begangen zu haben, Vorladungen von der Polizei erhalten oder von dieser gesucht werden."* - *"um die deutsche Seite für seinen Vorschlag geneigter zu machen, Verhandlungen über die Frage der Zahlung von Entschädigungen aufzunehmen."* BdBRD - SE - 204 Merten Ber. No. 608/58 of 14 June 1958: BA B141/9568, p. 13f.

In the middle of July it became known in Bonn that Tousis intended to spend his holidays in Germany and wanted to have a talk in Bonn. The AA agreed that he should be received but that the talks would have a totally private character.[1] On 30 July a first meeting took place in the BMJ (Ministry of Justice). Tousis stressed that the purpose of his visit was to get in contact with the appropriate authorities, *"in order find together a way to a solution of the existing difficulties."* He proposed official talks. His interlocutor replied that he would have to contact his superiors.[2] During his conversation in the AA Tousis stressed that the Greek Government would not use the Merten case to put pressure on the German side in the reparations question. The representative of the AA countered that the Merten case created a headache in Germany and strained the prosperous cooperation. The Federal Government would make an effort in autumn *"to help Greece especially economically. It would be negative, if parallel to the measures intended by us, in Athens an action would be sought which would here and there stir up the public opinion and would revive reminiscences of a time which both sides would not want."* The AA asked Tousis to consider whether the declaration of economic cooperation should cause a declaration of a general amnesty. Tousis, however, did not understand that the promise to help Greece economically was exactly that which he wanted only under a different denomination. He remained at his position and added threateningly that the Greek judges could not defy the law.[3] At the end Tousis gave the understanding that the trial against Merten would begin in November or December.[4]

In the beginning of September the negotiations about the credits began which were constantly strained by the Merten case. Both sides agreed that economic aid was a suitable means to forget the past. Bonn made the understanding that the Merten case could impair the granting of an economic aid because there was the danger that the parliament (Bundestag) might refuse the agreement if Merten was put to trial. The Greek side promised to seek a solution of the problem before the signing of the economic agreement.[5]

---

1 DBMdJ 9250/1-3-23292/58 on 23 July 1958; BA B141/9568, p. 33.

2 *"um gemeinsam einen Weg zur Lösung der bestehenden Schwierigkeiten zu finden."* DBMJ 9250/1-G on 30 July 1958: BA B141/9568, p. 38.

3 *"Griechenland wirtschaftlich in besonderem Maße unter die Arme zu greifen. Es sei daher schlecht, wenn Hand in Hand mit den von uns beabsichtigten Maßnahmen, in Athen ein Verfahren angestrebt würde, das drüben wie bei uns zweifellos die öffentliche Meinung in Wallung bringen würde und Reminiszenzen an eine Zeit hervorkehren würde, die von beiden Seiten sicherlich nicht gewünscht würden."* Spiliotis, *op. cit.*, p. 109.

4 *Ibidem*, p. 118.

5 *Ibidem*, p. 119.

On 10 November Karamanlis arrived in Bonn. The legal department of the AA had proposed that Chancellor Adenauer should hint that the German Government expected a transfer of Merten. Should the problem of the war crimes not be solved before the ratification of the economic agreement there could be difficulties in the Bundestag. [1]

On 12 November Adenauer and Karamanlis talked among other things also *"about the Greek manhunt against alleged German war criminals and especially the case of Merten."* Adenauer pointed to the actions of the Greek police against German tourists. Karamanlis declared *"that after his return to Athens he himself would look after this affair and would do everything to hinder any further disturbance of the German-Greek relations."*[2] On 13 November 1958 a confidential protocol was signed in which the questions of the German war criminals and of the German properties in Greece were regulated.[3]

It is interesting to note in this context that Konstantinos Svolopoulos in his 12 volumes edition of the archives of Karamanlis described the Bonn visit in detail and wrote about the credit of 200 million DM but the Merten case is not mentioned with a single word. The index of names of this many volume edition does not even contain the name of Merten.[4]

After his return to Athens Karamanlis ordered Foreign Minister, E. Averof. and the Minister in the Office of the Prime Minister, K. Tsatsos, to inform the German Embassy that the Merten case was finished by a special law and Merten himself would be transferred to the Federal Republic of Germany. At the end of November it was heard in the Greek News that the persecution of the war criminals had been stopped.[5] This declaration triggered a storm of protest in the Greek press. From *Estia* which was close to Markezinis to the EDA paper *Avgi,* even *Kathimerini* which was friendly to the Government, all papers were united in the rejection. On 2 December 1958 *Eleftheria* wrote that it

1 Lazaridou, *op. cit.*, p. 257.

2 *"über die griechischen Fahndungsmaßnahmen gegen angebliche deutsche Kriegsverbrecher und insbesondere über den Fall Merten."* - *"dass er nach seiner Rückkehr nach Athen sich selbst um die Angelegenheit kümmern werde und alles tun werde, um weitere Störungen der deutsch-griechischen Beziehungen zu vermeiden."* DBMJ -9250/1-3-23428/58 vom 18. November 1958: BA B 141/9568, p. 137f.

3 Seelos to AA on 11 December 1958: BA/ZWA B 141/9573, p. 26. Quoted from. Spiliotis, *op. cit.*, p. 120.

4 Konstantinos Svolopoulos (ed.), *Konstantinos Karamanlis. Archeio gegonota kai keimena,* Vol. III, *Oktaetia dimiourgias 1956-1963* (Athen: Idryma Konstantinos Karamanlis, 1994), pp. 271-302.

5 Spiliotis, *op. cit.*, p. 120.

would be unacceptable that persons who were on trial should be transferred to Germany. This would insult the national dignity.[1]

In January 1959 Karamanlis repeated his promise to Ambassador Kordt that the Merten case would be rectified by an act of grace,[2] but it was clear that the internal Greek pressure was increasing. During a private conversation with the new German Ambassador Seelos Karamanlis regretted that he could not keep his promise in the Merten case. The opposition in the cabinet was so strong that he could not complete his plan simply deport Merten to Germany. The trial had to be brought to a finish. He intended to have it begin soon and would try to influence the composition of the court to avoid a death sentence. After the judgement Merten would be deported as soon as possible. The German Government should not worry about the other 850 war crime cases.[3]

On 14 January 1959 the Greek Government submitted a draft law about the suspension of the persecution of war criminals which on 29 January was approved by parliament and was signed by the King on 18 February. It read: *"Now that the persecution of German citizens, which listed as war criminals, has began by the judicial authorities in their homeland, the persecution in Greece will be suspended except those cases in which the defendant is in a Greek jail and against whom decisions to bring him to court have been released."*[4] Thus Merten could bc brought to the court. He was the only defendant who was in a Greek prison. However the German Embassy and the AA realized that the formulation of the suspension was so vague that it was possible to continue arresting people. At the same time it was stated that the *"Greek Government was struggling to enfeeble the accusation that there was a connection between the treatment of the war criminal question and German credits."*[5]

1 Attachment to Embassy report of 4 December 1958: BA B 141/9573, p. 30f.

2 Aide Mémoire of 4 February 1959: BA B 141/9568, p. 137f.

3 Spiliotis, *op. cit.*, p. 121f.

4 *"Nachdem die Strafverfolgung deutscher Staatsangehöriger, die als Kriegsverbrecher geführt werden, seitens der Justizbehörden ihres Heimatlandes begonnen hat, wird die Strafverfolgung in Griechenland ausgesetzt (suspendiert), [...] ausgenommen diejenigen Fälle, bei denen die Angeklagten in Griechenland verwahrt werden und gegen dieselben bis zum Inkrafttreten dieses Gesetzes Verweisungsbeschlüsse [...] erlassen worden sind."* Translation of law No. 3933: BA B 141/9573, p. 168.

5 *"griechische Regierung bemüht sei, den Vorwurf zu entkräften, dass ein Zusammenhang zwischen der Behandlung der Kriegsverbrecherfrage und den deutschen Krediten besteht."* Botschaft an AA am 16. Januar 1959: BA B 141/9573, pp. 169f, 172f.

In early February it was suspected that Tousis had had his fingers in the game.[1] On 4 February the Embassy detected that Germany had been outwitted because on 5 November 1958 a second case had been opened against Merten which was not covered by the new law. The trial would begin on 11 February 1959. Thus *"the promise given by Prime Minister Karamanlis to chancellor Adenauer on 12 November 1958 in Bonn which was repeated in January to the German Ambassador that the Merten case would be finished by an act of grace after sentencing was made impossible because the pending second trial would be opposed to any act of grace."*[2]

The central legal protection department of the AA was of the opinion that this law had changed nothing. The problem of war criminals had not been solved. The reparations questions were still open. Merten's defence lawyer Kurt Walter expressed the opinion that *"the statement is justified that this law does not bring any progress, on the contrary it hinders the settlement a part of the cases by limitation of time."*[3]

The Athens Trial

By 21 February 1959 Merten had spent 21 months in solitary confinement in the Averof prison in Athens. On this date the trial began at a special military court. It had been decided that the trial should be in a military court because thus the government could control it more easily. The judges of a military court unlike their civilian colleagues were not obliged to check whether the testimonies of the witnesses for the prosecution or of witnesses for the defence were true. The chairman of the tribunal was colonel Ioannis Kokoretsas. He was a former collaborator, a sub-leader of Grivas' collaborating organization CHI (X) and a militant anti-Communist who had served as a judge in the military courts during the Greek civil war in which he behaved himself as horrible as Freisler on the notorious Nazi "Voksgerichtshof".[4] The minister of

1 BA B 141/9573, p. 174.

2 *"die Einhaltung des Bundeskanzler Adenauer am 12. November 1958 in Bonn von dem Ministerpräsidenten [Karamanlis] gegebenen und im Januar dem deutschen Botschafter gegenüber wiederholten Versprechen, dass nämlich der Fall Merten nach der Verurteilung durch einen Gnadenakt bereinigt werden würde, praktisch unmöglich gemacht, da nach Abschluss des ersten Verfahrens das noch schwebende zweite Verfahren jedem Gnadenakt entgegenstehen würde."* Aide Mémoire: BA B 141/9573, p. 176.

3 *"es berechtigt ist zu sagen, dass dieses Gesetz praktisch überhaupt keinen Fortschritt bringt, im Gegenteil es verhindert die Erledigung eines Teiles der Fälle durch Ablauf der Verjährung."* Walter an Zentrale Rechtsschutzstelle am 5. Februar 1959: BA B 141/9573, p. 174f.

4 Giorgios Dimitrakos, *Απολογισμός και απολογία "από του φοβερού βήματος..."* (Athen:

justice, K. Tsatsos, had instructed him to push the case through in two weeks and to reject all private plaintiffs. The first instruction failed because the proceedings lasted until 5 March. Kokoretsas complied with the second instruction already on the first day of the trial when he rejected all private suits. The real reason for the rejection may be found in the field of politics. Among the lawyers who represented Jewish interests was the well known leftist Ilias Tsirimokos of the EDA. Obviously the government wanted to avoid a situation in court that was completely out of control.[1]

In order to give an impression of the atmosphere of hate in which the trial took place an article of a Newspaper of Salonika (*Ellinikos Vorras*) shall be quoted: *"Like a lover revolves the house of his beloved a culprit does the same at the place of his crime. This psychological truth caused the former German commander of Salonika during the time of the occupation when Europe and our country moaned under the boots of the Third Reich to come to Greece ten days ago. He was not only the master of the property but of thousands of people. The Greeks were afraid to look into his face. Merten said this person will die and it did so or this person will live and it lived. He had the power of the Roman emperors and played the role of a Nero and Caligula. He was proud to say that Hitler was his friend and boasted that he was in close correspondence with him and all believed this because he had the characteristics of this. He was cunning, adroit, a diplomat, criminal and robber. He had the qualities to be a leading Nazi. His crimes have no begin and no end. For three days the investigating judge is in Salonika and listens to the witnesses. But the thousands who are dead now what will they testify."*[2]

Polytypo, 1991), pp. 175ff.

1 Spiliotis, *op. cit.*, p. 131f.

2 *"Wie der Liebhaber [...] das Haus der Geliebten umkreist, so der Täter den Ort des Verbrechens. Diese psychologische Wahrheit veranlasste vor zehn Tagen den ehemaligen deutschen Kommandanten von Saloniki während der Zeit der Besatzung, als Europa und unser Land unter dem Stiefel des Dritten Reiches stöhnten, nach Griechenland zu kommen. Er war nicht nur Herr über Vermögen, sondern über Tausende von Menschen. Die Griechen scheuten sich, ihm ins Gesicht zu sehen. Merten sagte, dieser wird sterben, und er starb, oder dieser wird leben, und er lebte. Er hatte die Macht römischer Kaiser und spielte die Rolle eines Nero und eines Caligula. Er freute sich, Hitler seinen Freund nennen zu können, und gab an, in enger Korrespondenz mit ihm zu stehen, und alle glaubten das, denn er hatte die Eigenschaften dazu. Er war listig, gewandt, ein Diplomat, Verbrecher und Räuber. Er besaß die Eigenschaften, ein führender Nazi zu sein. Seine Verbrechen sind ohne Anfang und Ende. Seit drei Tagen ist der Untersuchungsrichter hier (in Saloniki) und lädt die Zeugen vor. Doch die Tausende, die jetzt tot sind, wie werden sie aussagen."* Quoted from Dimitrios Apostolopoulos, *Die griechisch-deutschen Nachkriegsbeziehungen* (Frankfurt: Peter Lang, 2004), p.150f.

The newspaper *Makedonia* wrote the following day that Merten had been the master of death or life of the whole population of Macedonia. *"From a greater circle of persons he took money to let them free [...] Merten had the power to exchange people damned to death to exchange them with other in_nocent people."*[1] In general this slandering in the press is a common habit in Greece whenever the hate felt needs an outside target. Whether Merten enriched himself of Jewish property can be doubted but the opposite cannot be proven.

In Athens the newspapers showed more restraint. Influenced by the government they did not attack Germany but Merten was portrayed a criminal: *"It is decisive that Merten seems to belong to the first set of war criminals and that his different existence of today does not liberate him from his blood past."* In the eyes of this newspaper Merten was Hitler's administrator of Macedonia. The newspaper *To Vima* speculated whether Merten's crimes could not lead to a death sentence.[2] The hateful attacks went on for some weeks but then Tousis stopped them by an order.

Tousis main aim was the enforcement of the reparations claim. Apparently he was not informed that the 200 million DM investment credit was a disguised reparation. In order to avoid a release of Merten at the end of the first trial Tousis had seen to it that there would be a second trial. The Greek Government had intended that the trial would go off without a hitch but in the days before the trial began there had been a demagogic press campaign against Merten which heated the atmosphere. When on 11 February 1959 Merten in handcuffs was led up the outside staircase of the Athens District Court aggressive shouts were heard from a big crowd. The courtroom was packed full. Journalists from Greece and foreign countries observed the trial. Among the observers was the lawyer Dieter Posser of the law office of Gustav Heinemann in Essen.[3]

The Marbach Case

There had been four criminal counts which had to be dealt with. (1) The activities which led to the events on 11 July 1942 on the *Plateia Eleftherias* and

1 *"Von einem größeren Personenkreis nahm er für die Freilassung große Geldbeträge [...] Merten war befugt, die zum Tode Verurteilten gegen andere Unschuldige auszutauschen." Ibidem.*

2 *"Entscheidend ist, dass Merten zur ersten Garnitur der Kriegsverbrecher zu gehören scheint und dass seine wie auch immer geartete heutige Existenz ihn nicht von der Verantwortung für seine blutige Vergangenheit befreit." Ibidem*, p. 151.

3 Spiliotis, *op. cit.*, p. 131f.

to the expropriation of the Jewish cemetery of Thessalonika. (2) The transport of the Jews of Salonika to the extermination camps in Poland. (3) The shooting of 600 hostages and (4) the plundering of the shops in Salonika and the property of private citizens. Their value was said to amount to 1,5 million sovereigns.[1] These charges have been dealt with earlier. Since it is impossible to deal with each testimony we will take a closer look at the topics mentioned earlier. Additionally it must be taken into consideration that the documents of the trial were destroyed during the time of the military junta. As we described the facts in an earlier chapter we need not repeat them here once more.

However, the first criminal indictment was not confined to the events in Athens and to Merten alone but included his predecessor in office Dr. Karl Marbach. Merten wanted to prove that he had not been present in Athens when the events on the Freedom Square took place. He named his predecessor as main witness. In order to verify this with the help of the German Embassy in Athens and the Foreign Ministry in Bonn he contacted the legal authority of the German federal state of Schleswig-Holstein in June 1958. On 22 July 1958 Marbach appeared before the local district court (Amtsgericht) in Kiel.

Under oath Marbach made following statements: He could not remember Max Merten. Possibly he had met him once in the cafeteria. He himself did not transfer any of his competences to Merten but his deputy did because he had been elsewhere. He stressed that until his departure from Greece he had not heard of any reprisals measures. He had never heard anything about enforced labour especially not by Jews under the age of 45. He had never heard about the rounding up of the Jews on the Freedom Square (Plateia Eleftherias) on 11 July 1942. This statement he repeated twice as he did that he did not transfer his competence to Merten.[2]

These were straightforward lies which provoke the question why Marbach did not tell the truth and risked to tell lies under oath. The explanation is rather clear: If he had told the truth he would have admitted his crimes and would have encountered difficulties as high civil servant. He might even be taken to court. Therefore he pretended not to remember anything of the events. On the other hand Marbach did not help his successor Merten in Athens at all, on the contrary Marbach's statement reinforced the Greek allegations.

No wonder that Merten was infuriated. On 27 August 1958 he pressed criminal charges against an unknown person. In the text he refuted Marbach's

---

1 Apostolopoulos, *op. cit.*, p. 149.

2 Das Amtsgericht, Abt. 12 AR 745/58 of22 July 1958 Schleswig-Holsteinisches Landesarchiv Abt. 605 Nr. 3470

allegations in detail. For example, Merten described how he took over the office from Marbach himself. He stressed that Marbach had been in office for three weeks after his arrival in Salonika. He and Marbach had been together for weeks and they had had hours of conversation about the outstanding problems. During these conversations Marbach informed Merten about the events on the Freedom Square. By his decision - so Marbach - he had solved the Jewish problem since the Jews would not survive the murderous climate when building roads.

Merten then quoted a letter by *Sonderführer* and chief interpreter Arthur Meißner which the latter sent to Merten's wife which proves clearly that during the Freedom Square events Merten was not in Salonika and that Marbach's statements were lies. Merten closed his text by stating that he had filed his charges against an unknown person (meaning of course Marbach) hoping that he could include the result in his defence.[1]

A press release by the government of Schleswig-Holstein on 7 October 1958 shows clearly that the judicial authorities of this state had come to the conclusion that Merten had not been present in Salonika during the events of the Freedom Square. This had been proven by the statements of Dr. Parisius and chief interpreter Meixner. Parisius confirmed that he had travelled on the same train as Merten which arrived on 6 August 1942 in Salonika. Meixner stressed that he had accompanied Marbach on the Plateia Eleftherias on 11 July in his capacity as interpreter. Marbach himself repeated that he did not have "one atom" remembrance of those events.[2]

From another press release it becomes evident that the Schleswig-Holstein state attorney confirmed that Merten had not been in Salonika before August 1942. But the state attorney had not been able to find out who had been responsible for the orders given at that time. The investigations did not prove that the public officer of the state, Marbach, had been guilty Therefore the lawsuit against Marbach had been closed. Thus nothing could happen to Marbach in the Salonika case. But the case of the false oath was still open and there was a preliminary legal investigation of the the senior public prosecutor (Oberstaatsanwalt) Dr. Paul Thamm in Kiel.[3] During the Third Reich Thamm had been a member of the NSDAP and a typical Nazi jurist who had

---

1 Max Merten to the First State Attorney in Kiele on 27 August 1958. Schleswig-Holsteinisches Landesarchiv Abt. 605 Nr. 3470.

2 Pressestelle der Landesregierung Schleswig-Holstein on 7 October 1958. Schleswig-Holsteinisches Landesarchiv Abt. 605 Nr. 3470.

3 Entwurf einer Pressemitteilung on 28 January 1959. Schleswig-Holsteinisches Landesarchiv Abt. 605 Nr. 3470.

demanded numerous death sentences.[1] Already in 1946 the British authorities made him chief of the the state attorneys of Kiel. Now a new eyewitness of the events on the Plateia Elefherias appeared, Mrs Lisa Blumenfeld, who had accompanied Marbach on the Freedom Square. Thamm found an excellent excuse how to stop the persecution of Marbach: As it was impossible to find the truth in Kiel the Greek justice should be included in the procedure. [2] Thus the case was dragged on until Merten's return in 1960.

Among the witnesses of the defence were the delegate of the IRC René Burkhardt, the Italian Consul General in Salonika Guiseppe Castruccio and Merten's superior *Kriegsverwaltungsrat* of the Army Group E Theodor Parisius who was now press officer of the state government of Niedersachsen. They stated that the orders had been signed by Merten but not on his own initiative but these orders were orders ultimately given by Hitler. The Governor General of Macedonia Simonidis, also, spoke positively about Merten. Parisius was able to prove from his diary that in July 1942 Merten had still been in Germany and could not have been on the Plateia Eleftherias.[3]

Burkhardt had come from Manila to Athens, where he lived then, to help Merten. He confirmed the story of the effort to evacuate the Jews to Palestine.[4] General Chrysochoou made the following statement; *"Merten was a gentleman. When after these words of the witness of the prosecution there were loud disapproving signs of the public he stated once more; 'I remain, Merten was a gentleman."*[5]

One fact, however, should be recalled here: Merten was a civil servant associated to the Wehrmacht who did not have any military authority. He could never have given an order to shoot hostages. Such orders were given by commissioned officers of the Wehrmacht. Moreover it should be noted that from the third order on of the deportation of the Jews he signed "i. A." (im Auftrag

1 Ernst Klee: *Das Personenlexikon zum Dritten Reich. Wer war was vor und nach 1945.* (Koblenz, 2011), p. 621.
2 Letter by Thamm to the investigating judge in Kiel, Schleswig-Holsteinisches Landesarchiv Abt. 605 Nr. 3470.
3 Kralowa, *op. cit.*, p. 159f.
4 *Hamburger Echo* (20. September 1960), p. 8
5 *"'Merten war ein Herr'. Als nach diesen Worten des Zeugen der Anklage Mißfallenskundgebungen des Publikums laut wurden, erklärte er noch einmal: 'Ich bleibe dabei, Merten war ein Herr'." Ibidem.*

- on order of) meaning the WB Saloniki-Ägäis, general Krenzki. Thus he made it clear that not he was responsible but the general.[1]

There were 100 witnesses of the prosecution and 50 of the defence. The trial had three phases. During the first, from 11 to 18 February, the witnesses of the prosecution were heard. They were able to tell invented stories or even straight forward lies without any risk because the truth of their statement was not verified. On 19 and 20 February the Greek defence witnesses were heard and from 20 to 25 February the foreign witnesses. Afterwards Merten was heard.

The Verdict

The military prosecutor had demanded a total punishment of 140 years jail for all individual cases which was reduced to a realistic 20 years jail sentence. The verdict of 5 March 1959 came to a total of 125 years which were concentrated and reduced to 25 years prison and to the confiscation of Merten's properties.[2] The German Embassy sent a report on the reactions of the Greek public in Athens: *"The verdict caused a great surprise. Especially in the circles of Greek jurists there was indignation. Generally it had been expected that there would be a verdict between acquittal and at most eight years of prison. Generally the verdict cannot be brought in line with the taking of evidence and the whole procedure of the trial."* An explanation was not expected even when the text of the judgement was submitted in writing. In the Greek military judiciary explanatory statements do not exist nor delines of argument. The judgement consisted only of a statement of the penalty.[3]

This kind of conduct of a case reminds one of the trials against the Left after the Dekemvriana when only incriminating arguments and no exonerating ones were noted. The verdicts in trials of the Civil War times had the same character. From the beginning of the trial the judgement was already fixed.

Lawyer Posser who had observed the trial, informed Heinemann about the judgement. Both considered it a total judicial wrongdoing. In their eyes the

1 Facsimiles of these letters with i. A. in Molho, *In Memoriam*, pp. 135-145.

2 Botschaft an AA 503-88 No. 381/1959 Anlage vom 6. März 1959; AA Referat 206 Band Nr. 135; Breyer, *op. cit.*, pp. 120-123.

3 *"Das Urteil hat hier große Überraschung ausgelöst. Besonders in Kreisen der griechischen Juristen war man zum Teil sogar empört. Allgemein hatte man damit gerechnet, dass ein Urteil ergehen würde, das zwischen Freispruch und höchstens acht Jahren Freiheitsstrafe liegen würde. Insbesondere lässt sich das Urteil mit dem Ergebnis der Beweisaufnahme und der ganzen Durchführung des Verfahrens einfach nicht in Einklang bringen."* Botschaft an AA 503-88 No. 381/1959 vom 6. März 1959; AA Referat 206 Band Nr. 135.

judgement was a crass contradiction of the facts. In a letter to the Bundestag budget committee MP Heinemann demanded that the financial agreement should be sent back.[1] Obviously Heinemann had recognized the connection between the Merten case and the payment of disguised reparations.[2]

However Merten did not only get into the twilight of the final solution. As he was the "interface" between the Wehrmacht and the Greek administration and the population, he was responsible for their provisioning. He was the person who was noticed by the Greek population no wonder that they called him the "archont" or king of Salonika. Because the accusations of corruption are based on hearsay they must not be taken seriously. If one had not met Merten personally it is difficult to state whether he was honest and overstrained or an enigmatic character as it is often heard. Allegedly he did not come out of the events with a totally clean record, who, however, came out during that period. It cannot be excluded that the Greeks simply projected the behaviour of Greek bureaucrats onto Merten. Merten, however, was not the war criminal as he is described to this day.

However one can understand Samuel Hassid when he writes: *"Although our notion of his powers may be exaggerated, Merten cannot be considered innocent in the eyes of most of us Greek Jews. He might not have participated in the most heinous of Holocaust crimes, but he was directly involved in the destruction of our community. More distressing, however, than the case per se is the feeling that justice was not served in the case of Greece and its citizens (Jews, but also Christians ...) - which makes the Merten case a symbol. If one accepts his defence that he was not responsible for most of the crimes attributed to him, one must simultaneously acknowledge the fact that almost none of those allegedly responsible were punished either..."*[3]

Later he wrote: *"I am sure we all agree though that something is wrong somewhere: for the murder of the appr. 70,000 Jews in Greece, nobody paid any price!!!"*[4] Unfortunately this statement of Hassid is right. Alois Brunner, alias Alois Schmaldienst, was able to go into hiding in Germany until 1954, and when arrest threatened, he fled to Syria under the name of Georg Fischer with the help of BND chief Reinhard Gehlen. In Syria he worked for the BND and

---

1 ZRS-Aufzeichnung über Unterredung mit Heinemann und Posser mit AA- und ZRS-Vertretern am 8. April 1959 vom 10. April 1959: AA Referat 206 Band Nr. 134; Spiliotis, *op. cit.*, p. 134.

2 Burger speaks of economic agreement and does not understand that these payments were diguised reparations. Burger, *op. cit.*, p. 3.

3 Samuel Hassid, *The Trial of Max Merten in the Changing Mirrors of Time and Place* (Technion Haifa, 2002).

4 http://www.yvelia.com/kolhakehila/board/jews_greece_wwii/jews_greece_wwii.html.

in 1960 he became chief advisor of the Syrian government on Jewish questions. The Israeli secret service tried to kill him two times but did not succeed in doing this. Brunner lived unmolested in Damascus and even gave interviews to German and Austrian journalists. He died im December 2009.[1]

Wisliceny, on the other side, continued his horrible work until the end of the war. His last victims were the Hungarian Jews. In the Nuremberg Trial he was a witness for the prosecution. His statements were even used in the Eichmann trial in Jerusalem in 1961. After the end of the Nuremberg Trial he was extradited to the ĈSSR where in 1948 he was put to trial, sentenced to death and executed in February 1948. Eichmann's fate is known. Two of the main culprits did not escape punishment though not by Greek courts.

Apostolopoulos is right when he writes: *"Nevertheless the assumption of the Federal Government and the German public that there is a connection between the arresting of Merten and the economic desires of Greece is not wrong. Indeed one cannot deny a targeted political action of the Greek Government which was accompanied by a mobilisation of he public opinion. The fact that the Greek Government constantly articulated the wish, which becomes obvious from the documents, not to disturb the excellent relations with Germany while at the same time it used the pretext not to be able to intervene in the judicial process strengthens the impression that it was a staging."*[2]

Spiliotis comes to a slightly different conclusion when she writes: *"Merten's punishment was intended to assuage public opinion by showing the willingness of the Greek state to punish war criminals severely. This was the image that the Karamanlis government wished to project. We know, however, that at the very same moment, Merten's amnesty had been decided. Karamanlis had never planned to hold Merten in a Greek jail. He was simply awaiting the appropriate, favourable circumstances for his release."*[3] She mentions the

---

1 https://de.wikipedia.org/wiki/Alois_Brunner

2 *"Gleichwohl entbehrte die Annahme der Bundesregierung und der deutschen Öffentlichkeit, es bestehe ein Zusammenhang zwischen der Verhaftung Mertens und den wirtschaftlichen Wünschen Griechenlands, nicht der Plausibilität. In der Tat ist eine gezielte politische Aktion der griechischen Regierung, flankiert durch die Mobilisierung der öffentlichen Meinung, kaum zu leugnen. Die Tatsache, dass die griechische Regierung immer wieder, wie aus dem Akten hervorgeht, den Wunsch artikulierte, die ausgezeichneten Beziehungen zu Deutschland nicht zu stören, während sie sich gleichzeitig des Vorwandes bediente, nicht in den Gang der Justiz eingreifen zu können, bestärkt den Eindruck, dass es sich um eine Inszenierung handelte."* Apostolopoulos, *op. cit.*, p. 156.

3 Susanne-Sophia Spiliotis, "'An Affair of Politics, Not Justice' The Merten Trial (1957-1959) and Greek-German Relations", in: Mark Mazower (ed.), *After the War Was Over. Reconstructing the Family, Nation and State in Greece, 1943-1960* (Princeton: UP, 2000), p. 298.

compensations of the Global Agreement for those who had been victims of Nazi ideology but not the reparations.

A GDR Intervention

During the whole Merten affair the GDR (East Germany- DDR) had supplied incriminating evidence against Merten and the Federal Republic.[1] In March 1959 a group of Left and liberal deputies of the Greek parliaments travelled to the GDR. Allegedly Ulbricht offered reparation payments if Greece recognized the GDR. West-Germany would only pay compensations to victims of racial and religious persecution.[2] Whether or not this offer was initiated by Ulbricht is not known. But it is clear that such an offer would never be accepted by the right wing ERE Government. After all Greece was a member of NATO and there was the Hallstein doctrine. Thus, the East German Government could make this offer without any risk because it would be rejected. It was a propaganda manoeuvre aimed at diminish the reputation of West Germany and strengthen the EDA in their fight against the Greek Government. Besides that, the recipients of the DDR reparation payments would have been only former EAM/ELAS members i.e. leftists.

But the GDR offensive was not confined to transferring incriminating material against Merten to the EDA because EDA asked for material against Karamanlis, Makris and the future "neutral" member of the Cypriot High Court, Ernst Forsthoff which might be used against them.[3] In November 1959 the EDA deputy Komninos Pyromaglou, appeared in East-Berlin to obtain material against Merten. He promised to send a list with 300 war criminals to the GDR so that they could search for incriminating material.[4] Such contacts continued in 1960 as is proven by the GDR visit of the deputy Michail Kyrkos.[5]

Negotiations about Compensations and Merten's Release

In the summer of 1956 eleven Western European states jointly asked the FRG government to pay compensation for false imprisonment of persecuted persons of the Nazis (i.e. not for forced labourers or resistance fighters). In December 1958 Bonn informed these countries that the FRG war ready to nego-

---

1 Andreas Stergiou, *Im Spagat zwischen Solidarität und Realpolitik. Die Beziehungen zwischen der DDR und Griechenland und das Verhältnis der SED zur KKE* (Möhnesee: Bibliopolis, 2001), p. 99.

2 Spiliotis, *op. cit.*, p. 136f.

3 Deutsch-griechische Beziehungen in den 1950ziger Jahren, MfAA, A 2185, p. 19.

4 Note on a conversation between the Greek deputy Pyromaglou and the "Koll.[egen] Richter", Sektion Griechenland am 18. 11. 59. MfAA, A 12480.

5 *Ibidem*, p. 109.

tiate this question. However the provisions of the London Debt Agreement must not be violated and the financial abilities of the FRG must not be overstrained. It was stressed that the payments were voluntary.[1]

On 8 December 1958 the German government signalled Greece in a diplomatic note that it was ready to start negotiations about compensations.[2] The topics of these negotiations were not reparations and war crimes as in the negotiations in November 1956 but the compensation of crimes due to racist motives the so-called global agreement (Globalabkommen).[3]

On 18 February 1959 the law of the suspension of the criminal prosecution of war criminals became law. However, the word amnesty was not included in the text of the law. On 5 March 1959 Merten was sentenced to 25 years in prison. Though the Greek Government had promised to release Merten soon after the judgement, however, in May 1959 he was still in prison though ambassador Seelos had intervened with Karamanlis several times. Ambassador Ypsilantis gave to understand that they were waiting for a suitable moment then the release could be managed without great excitement of the public.[4] However, it is quite possible that Merten was kept in prison to be able to exert pressure during the negotiations about the compensations which were just beginning.[5]

Before the first round of negotiations in May 1959 Bonn asked the eight governments for the precise numbers of their demands. At the same time the German Embassies in these countries were ordered to start researches. The numbers which Greece submitted, in the eyes of the AA appeared too high and too unspecified when they compared them with publicly accessible data. During the first round of the negotiations from 4 to 6 May, the Greek side tried to push through a maximum demand of compensations for 190.800 former persecuted persons. It was obvious that this number included resistance fighters and other persons for which there would be no compensations. However, the Greek government did exactly try to do this. While Athens tried

---

1 Hagen Fleischer/Despina Konstantinakou, "Ad calendas graecas", pp. 375-457.

2 Spiliotis, *op. cit.*, p. 149.

3 "Globalentschädigungsabkommen: Verteilung an *"zugunsten der aus Gründen der Rasse, des Glaubens oder der Weltanschauung von nationalsozialistischen Verfolgungsmaßnahmen betroffenen Staatsangehörigen, die durch diese Verfolgungsmaßnahmen Freiheitsschäden oder Gesundheitsschädigungen erlitten haben, sowie besonders auch zugunsten der Hinterbliebenen der infolge dieser Verfolgungsmaßnahmen Umgekommenen."* http://www.auswaertiges-amt.de/DE/Aussenpolitik/InternatRecht/Entschaedigung_-node.html

4 Spiliotis, *op. cit.*, p. 138.

5 *Ibidem*, p. 140.

to push the number as high as possible Bonn tried to lower it. Bonn believed that about 10,000 Jews had survived the war who were entitled to to ask for compensations for racial persecution. In Greece nobody had lost his life for religious reasons. Ideological reasons referred to the communists but most of them had lost their lives during of resistance actions.[1]

Thus, the first negotiation round brought forth no result. The different opinions about the groups which might get a compensation intensified. Therefore the German side demanded a list of persecuted people with details about the reasons of the detention and its length in order to calculate the entitlements. The negotiations should be suspended until this list was submitted.[2]

On 17 October 1959 the Greek government submitted a draft law to the rump parliament by which all German war criminal cases should be definitely suspended without any exception. The opposition criticised this as a violation of the constitution. A rump parliament[3] could not release such a bill which was relevant for internal and external policy. It demanded that this bill be discussed by the full parliament. Because this would have meant publicity and excitement the ERE majority of the rump parliament rejected it. The bill provided an immediate stop of all cases against war criminals and their persecution and the release of all those imprisoned and their deportation. The latter concerned Merten. Additionally the national war criminal office was to be dissolved.[4] As in the law of 18 February 1959 the word amnesty was missing in the text. The opposition accused the government of colluding with the Germans. When criticism in the ERE-party began Foreign Minister Averof also told the deputies that the negotiation about the compensation agreement was running very well.[5]

During the violent parliamentary debate of the compensation bill it became clear that the law was closely linked with the reparations payment and the release of Merten. On 23 October 1959 the bill passed with a majority of the ERE votes. EDA voted against it. On 3 October it became a law. On 5 October Merten was deported to Germany. On 30 October ambassador Seelos admonished Bonn: *"A speedy positive solution of the reparation of Nazi victims question is now of acute importance otherwise the the aimed at psychological*

1 Fleischer, *Calendas*, pp. 402-405.

2 Spiliotis, *op. cit.*, p. 138.

3 In the summer pause only a very reduced pariament, the so-called rump parliament met. The King and the Government had prolonged this summer pause by one months in order to avoid a debate in the plenum. Fleischer, *Calendas,* p. 408.

4 Spiliotis, *op. cit.*, p. 141.

5 Spiliotis, *op. cit.*, p. 141.

effect of law, to end the question of the war criminals on both sides, might turn into the opposite."[1]

The Global Agreement

The German embassy in Athens worriedly observed the inner Greek discussion which became more and more heated and advised the AA to compensate the victims of sanctions as well: *"The psychological effect of our voluntary payment [would] be strongly impaired [...] if villages like Kalavryta and Distomon would not be considered at all. Besides that the barbarian slaughters committed by SS-units among the innocent inhabitants of numerous Greek villages when partisans were observed in their vicinity. were not agreed by any martial law but were typical national socialist wrong and we must have no interest in having these measures declared as such."*[2]

At the same time the Greek side made an effort to get a free hand in the distribution of the money received. Averof warned that otherwise the money would go to the Jews and the Communists. Seelos was skeptical about this demand. He considered the method practised in other countries to keep away from the distribution of the money to be wrong in Greece. If Germany did not have a say in distribution of the money it might *"be misused for ones own political purpose."*[3]

In the AA voices were heard which were in favour of compensating the victims of the mass retaliation actions such as Kalavryta and Distomon because these had not been military measures but measures based on the Nazi ideology. However those responsible saw this differently. Hints were made to

---

1 *"Eine baldige positive Regelung der Frage der Entschädigung von Naziopfern, ist daher jetzt von akuter Bedeutung, wenn die mit dem Gesetz zur Beendigung der Kriegsverbrecherfrage von beiden Seiten angestrebte psychologische Wirkung nicht in ihr Gegenteil umschlagen soll."* Spiliotis, *op. cit.*, p. 143f.

2 *"Die psychologische Wirkung unserer freiwilligen Zahlung [würde] stark beeinträchtigt [...], wenn Ortschaften wie Kalavryta und Distomon überhaupt nicht berücksichtigt werden. Im übrigen dürfte es sich bei den zum Teil barbarischen mit keinem Kriegsrecht zu vereinbarenden Metzeleien, die deutsche SS-Einheiten unter den unschuldigen Bewohnern zahlreicher griechischer Ortschaften veranstaltet haben, in deren Nähe Partisanentätigkeit beobachtet worden war, doch tatsächlich um ausgesprochen nationalsozialistisches Unrecht handeln und dürften wir jedes Interesse daran haben, dass diese Maßnahmen als solche angesehen werden."* Fleischer, *Calendas*, p. 413f. Kalavryta was a crime committed by the Wehrmacht. Hermann Frank Meyer, *Von Wien nach Kalavryta. Die blutige Spur der 117. Jäger-Division durch Serbien und Griechenland* (Mannheim: Bibliopolis, 2002).

3 *"allzusehr für eigene politische Zwecke missbraucht werden."* Fleischer, *Calendas*, p. 413.

Athens in January 1960 that the negotiations of Greece in regard to an association with the EWG (European Economic Community) should not be burdened with excessive compensation demands.[1]

The Ministry of Finance considered the Greek demands as exaggerated. Til the end of 1958 the Federal Government had believed that 100 million DM would be sufficient to satisfy the demands of all Western states. However Greek demand alone was double than that. The Ministry of Finance estimated the realistic Greek demands to be 65 million DM and opposed the political considerations of the AA to show themselves as generous to the Greeks. In February 1960 the undersecretary of the AA, Albert van Scherpenberg, urged the Ministry of Finance: He considered it necessary to make on offer to the Greek government which it could present to the parliament and the opposition. One should not frustrate the Greek public. The negotiations should be speeded up.[2]

In mid-February 1960 the next round of negotiations took place. The Greek side rejected the 60 million DM offered by the BMF as much too low. The Greek public had expected 200 million DM but would be satisfied with a sum between 130 and 150 million DM. Foreign Minister von Brentano had allegedly mentioned 120 million DM to Averof. Only such a sum could take the wind out of the opposition's sails. The representative of the Ministry of Finance tried to block this by stating that he did not know this. Scherpenberg, however, understood that action was needed and turned to his colleague of the BMF, Karl Hettlage. He told him about the negative consequences of a low offer: Karamanlis would not loose face when he mentioned the number in parliament and this was to be avoided. Also the German embassy in Athens warned against a sum much lower than 120 million DM. This would trigger a huge hate campaign. But the BMF continued to block. They did not want to surpass the sum of 65 million DM.[3]

Finally ambassador Ypsilantis asked for a meeting with Adenauer. It is not known what was said during this meeting but after the end of it the chancellor called together a special meeting of the cabinet. The AA and the BMF prepared statements. During the meeting on 2 March mainly Adenauer, Brentano and Hettlage spoke. Since the Minister of Finance did not support Hettlage he fought his last stand but then Adenauer intervened. The cabinet decided that the negotiations with the Greeks should continue on the basis of 100 million.

1 *Ibidem*, p. 414.
2 Spiliotis, *op. cit.*, p. 147.
3 Fleischer, *Calendas*, p. 417f.

Should the Greeks demand more then the maximum would be 115 million DM.[1]

Now a new poker round began. The Greek side insisted on 120 million. On the following day the German side slowly increased the sum but offering resistance. Finally on 9 March 1960 the sum of 115 million DM was agreed upon which would be paid in four installments. On 18 March the German-Greek Global Agreement was signed. Thus in four days the sum had been doubled. During the negotiations of the global agreement with the other Western states such a thing did not happen. It was a unique case.[2]

Article 1 of the agreement read that Germany paid Greece 115 million DM *"In favour of those Greek citizens which were hurt by national socialist persecution measure out of racial, religious or ideological reasons. The distribution of the amount is left to the discretion of royal Greek Government."* Article 2 stated that the sum would be paid in four installments. The last one would be paid on 1 March 1963. Article 3 stated clearly that with this payment *"all questions forming this treaty between the FRG and the Kingdom of Greece [are] terminally regulated."* At the end of the text it was stated that the agreement did not need any ratification. In an accompanying text it was stated that the Bonn government acted on the assumption that the Greek government would *"will in the future not demand regulations of further questions based on national-socialist measures of persecutions during the war and occupation time."* In his reply ambassador Ypsilantis agreed in the name of his government but precluded the right that if according to the London Debt Agreement the two Germanies were re-united new demands of reparations could be raised.[3] In the view of the then existing situation the question of reparations was closed for ever. A reunification of the two inimical Germanies was considered impossible.

When the negotiations of the Global Agreement were on the homestretch Merten could be released without taking a risk. Merten was the bargaining

---

1 *Ibidem*, p. 418f.

2 *Ibidem*, p. 419f.

3 *"zugunsten der aus Gründen der Rasse, des Glaubens oder der Weltanschauung von nationalsozialistischen Verfolgungsmaßnahmen betroffenen griechischen Staatsangehörigen. Die Verteilung des Betrages bleibt dem Ermessen der Königlichen Griechischen Regierung überlassen."* - *"alle den Gegenstand dieses Vertrages bildenden Fragen im Verhältnis der Bundesrepublik Deutschland zu dem Königreich Griechenland [...sind] abschließend geregelt"* - *"künftig an sie mit dem Verlangen nach Regelung weiterer Fragen, die aus nationalsozialistischen Verfolgungsmaßnahmen während Kriegs- und Besatzungszeit herrührten, nicht herantreten wird."* *Bundesgesetzblatt* (1961) II, p. 1597f.

chip in both negotiations. Spiliotis is right when she wrote: *"Merten was the bargaining chip of the Greeks for their option on reparations."*[1]

The Distribution of the 115 Million DM

According to the ideas of the Bonn government the means of the Global Compensation were primarily to be distributed among the racial persecuted persons. But it had been accepted that also victims of hostage executions and massacres of the Wehrmacht and the SS should be compensated. Like in all other global agreements the German government had agreed that the distribution should be made by the relevant governments. This functioned well in all Western European countries and the means were distributed in a just manner. Greece, however, was different because of its clientelistic system. Right from the beginning it had been clear that persons who had claims and were close to ERE would be preferred.[2] Furthermore the Jews would not be indemnified to the degree it could be expected because they still were second class citizens. Jews who were close to EDA would remain empty handed. They were not even informed about the possibilities as I was informed by leftist Jews during a conference in Thessaloniki in 1991.

During the negotiations of the Global Compensation the representative of the Central Council of Jews, Constant, had several times suggested *"to provide a stipulation in the treaty which defines the sums for the racial persecuted and to oblige the Greek to use this sum also for the Jews who had survived."*[3] Constant knew that the entitlement of many Jew to receive payment of compensation was dubious. The BMJ saw this also. In an internal expertise they came to the conclusion that many of the claimants being "allogenes" were not entitled at all. However the 4,000 surviving Jews were entitled to 10,8 million DM, i.e. 150 DM per month for 18 months. The BMJ emphasized to Constant that the 115 million DM were exclusively for the Jews. Since Constant did not succeed in adding the proposed clause the Greek government

1 "Merten war das Faustpfand der Griechen für ihre Option auf Entschädigungszahlungen." Spiliotis, *op. cit.*, p. 155.

2 Fleischer, *Calendas*, p. 428. *"Die Opposition befürchtete nicht nur eine Kungelei der regierungsparteilich verfilzten Administration zugunsten von Antragstellern mit 'rechter' Gesinnung, sondern auch Abzweigungen für obskure Entwicklungsprojekte."*

3 *"in den Vertrag eine Bestimmung aufzunehmen, die die für die rassisch Verfolgten in Betracht kommende Summe ausweist und der griechischen Regierung die Auflage zu machen, diese Summe auch für die überlebenden Juden Griechenlands zu verwenden."* Spiliotis, *op. cit.*, p. 150f.

could extend the compensation to other groups as well. Therefore the Greek Jews received only 59 percent of the money granted to them by courts.[1]

However not only were the Jews cheated but also the Greek victims of German retaliatory measures. Originally 35,000 Drachmae should be paid for each violent death (1 DM = 7,5 Drachmae).[2] In the case of Kalavryta 32,000 Drachmae were paid which was a considerable sum because a teacher earned 1,100 Drachmae per month. At the end each family received 17,000 Drachmae though in many cases more than one male family member had been killed. More was promised but nothing came any more. The distribution of the money was carried out by the government according to the principle of clientelism i.e only the members of the government's party were supported. Villages in which the EDA had obtained the majority of the votes at the last election received nothing.[3] In Distomon the families of victims came off better because the families received a compensation for each family member killed. The data of the total sum stretched from 8,000 to 39,000 Drachmae. For each victim 8-10,000 Drachmae were paid.[4]

A former member of the German Embassy in Athens told me some years ago that only the first rate was distributed by the Greek government, i.e. 35 million DM. The justification was incredible: There were too many claims for compensation. Allegedly large parts were used to close the chronic holes in the Greek budget. In a letter to me he wrote: *"More details about the division of the 115 millions is unknown to me; then there were rumours that the politicians were quarrelling among each other because each of them wanted the greatest part for his own constituency. Always the same 'story'. These rumours circulated in the embassy also."*[5]

1 *Ibidem*, pp. 150-152.

2 Fleischer, *Calendas*, p. 429.

3 Hermann Frank Meyer, Von Wien nach Kalavryta. Die blutige Spur der 117. Jäger-Division durch Serbien und Griechenland, (Mannheim: Bibliopolis, 2002), p. 484.

4 This information was obtained by Brigitte Spuller from citizens of Distomon. Frau Spuller organized from 1986 tils 2012 the regular meetings of the youth of the evangelische Kirche in Nürnberg and Distomon. 1990 the towns of Distomon made her an honorary citizen. Frau Spuller was decorated for her reconciliation work with the Bundesverdienstkreuz. In the meantime she is attacked by certain people - without any reason.

5 *"Näheres über die Verteilung der 115 Mio. ist mir nicht bekannt, es gingen damals Gerüchte um, dass die Politiker untereinander zankten, denn jeder wollte den größten Teil für seinen eigenen Wahlbezirk in Anspruch nehmen. Immer die gleiche 'Story'. Diese Gerüchte kursierten damals auch in der Botschaft."* Letter to me on 23 June 2016.

Merten's Release

The World Jewish Congress in London protested vigorously against Merten's release from the Greek prison. Seen from London Merten was a war criminal and the director of this institution, A. L. Easterman was of the opinion that Merten had gotten away too cheaply with his two and a half year jail. He demanded from the German Federal Government to do everything possible to punish Merten. Should this not be done it would become *"another scandal affecting Germany's still far from firm standing as a democratic country."* [1]

When Merten arrived by plane in the evening of 5 November 1959 in Munich he was arrested on the basis of a warrant of arrest by the Berlin district court of 7 October 1957 and brought to the Moabit prison the next day. The investigating judge interviewed him on 6, 10, 11 and 12 November and released him from pre-trial custody on 16 November.[2] However, this was not the end, but the beginning of a new judicial round.

1 Spiliotis, *op. cit.*, p. 153.
2 ZStL 508 AR-Z139/59 Prozessgeschichte, p. 3f.

MERTEN'S FIGHT FOR REHABILITATION

Merten's Fight with Globke

Merten's life after his return was influenced by his fight for rehabilitation. On the one hand he had to fight against the war crime trial initiated against him. On the other hand he tried to attack the Bonn Government in the person of Adenauer's undersecretary of state, Hans Globke who had let him run into the knife in Athens and had not done enough to bring him out. Besides that he settle his score with the Greek Government by attacking Karamanlis and Makris.

During the months following his release from the Moabit prison. the files of the Greek trial were translated and the investigating magistrate heard eleven German witnesses. In mid-1960 Merten wanted to interrogate Greek witnesses in Athens but the BMJ advised against this. Thereupon in February 1961 the magistrate invited 14 Greek witnesses to Berlin but only one appeared. Now he tried on the basis of a request for judicial assistance to have witnesses questioned in Athens but this was rejected by the Greeks without giving any reason. When he invited 30 other witnesses from Athens only 4 appeared. Efforts of the German consulate in Thessaloniki to view the files there failed because they could not be found. Finally it was agreed that Greek judges would examine the witnesses in Greece a process which required an enormous amount of time. As late as April 1966 the protocols of these examinations arrived in Berlin. In May 1966 the Berlin prosecution took over the later investigations and on 4 June 1968 closed the proceedings against Merten. As his innocence had not been proven beyond reason of doubt Merten had to bear the cost of the case. The order to dismiss the case had a remarkable 438 pages.[1]

Merten's quarrel with Globke already began while he was waiting for his trial in Athens. He had told the court that Globke had torpedoed the transport of the Jewish women and children to Palestine. The Embassy tried to stop him from stating this: *"Never anybody said, you may not. The members of the Embassy argued instead: Mr. Merten the Federal Republic takes all trouble and in four weeks you will be free. Do not trigger a new avalanche."* [2]

---

1 ZStL 508 AR-Z139/59 Prozessgeschichte, pp. 4-8.

2 *"Nie hat jemand gesagt, das dürfen Sie nicht. Die Vertreter der Botschaft argumentierten vielmehr: Herr Merten, die Bundesrepublik gibt sich doch alle Mühe, und in vier Wochen sind Sie ja draußen. Lösen Sie doch keine neue Lawine aus."* Merten, however, made his statement."Globke. Ein unbedeutender Mann" *Der Spiegel* 8 (15. Februar 1961), p.23.

As soon as March 1960 Merten's lawyer Dieter Posser from Essen had contacted the Hessian Chief Public Prosecutor Fritz Bauer. Bauer stemmed from a German-Jewish family that had fled abroad in time from the Nazi persecution abroad, Bauer returned to Germany after the end of the war and in the 1950s and 1960s he did his best to bring those responsible for the holocaust especially those from the concentration camps to court. With the first Auschwitz trial (1963-1965) he opened the judicial process of dealing with the Nazi crimes. Bauer carefully listened to Posser's story about Merten and on 3 June 1960 Merten told his story during an informal conversation with Bauer. Bauer took Merten's story so seriously that he wrote a note with the reference number I Ar/26/60 Gsta, but he did not yet open a case against Globke.[1]

On 19 July 1960 Merten was called to the district court (*Amtsgericht*) Tiergarten in Berlin to be interrogated by the judge there. Merten insisted that he needed an official permission from Bonn to testify. Bauer asked for this in Bonn and the permit was given on 7 September 1960 by the Federal Ministry of Justice (BMJ). However, Merten was neither heard in Frankfurt nor in Berlin.[2]

This, however, was not enough for Merten. He addressed the Hamburg newspaper *Hamburger Echo*, which was close to the SPD. The newspaper published his story in a series of article series from 12 September to 3 October. The article of 17 September contained the story how Globke hindered the transport of the Jewish women and children to Palestine. On 28 September the *Hamburger Echo* published a letter by Globke on the first page in which he unintentionally confirmed Merten's story - just as the author of the had stated. On 29 September *Der Spiegel* repeated the accusations against Globke.[3]

However, Globke was not content to write that letter to the editor. Together with chancellor Adenauer he pressed charges against Merten on account of slandering and wrong accusations before the Office of Public Prosecutor in Bonn. Obviously Globke also wanted revenge. Before however Merten could be heard by the Frankfurt court he had to appear in the prosecutor's office in Bonn and was heard.[4]

During two afternoons Globke was interviewed by Werner Pfromm, the Bonn Public Prosecutor, who himself had a Nazi past as NS controlling offi-

1 Bevers, *op. cit.*, p. 169.
2 "Globke. Ein unbedeutender Mann" *Der Spiegel* 8 (15. Februar 1961), p. 22.
3 "Kriegsverbrechen Griechenland. Ihr Onkel Konstantin" *Der Spiegel* 40 (28. September 1960), p. 32.
4 "Globke. Ein unbedeutender Mann" *Der Spiegel* 8 (15. Februar 1961), p.22.

cer. Globke declared that he had had no part in the German anti-Jewish laws. He had allegedly been the most unimportant civil servant in the ministry of the interior.[1] After Merten had been interviewed by the Bonn Public Prosecutor, Fritz Bauer opened proceedings against Globke which were transferred to Bonn. Before the proceedings were moved there, Adenauer had written a letter to prime minister of Hessia August Zinn which allegedly was not sent. Its wording is typical for that time: *"The Communist campaign of defamation against leading personalities in the Federal Republic, which concentrates lately on undersecretary of state Dr, Globke has entered a new stage to my great regret because of the recents events in Frankfurt/M. For the first time the Ulbricht regime succeeded to give the material, used during its well known attacks on Dr, Globke , to a high ranking organ of the state, general attorney Bauer. According to newspaper reports they declared their satisfaction, that general attorney Bauer, whose objectivity I do not doubt at all, was drawn into a twilight and also the trial will become political. Nothing could be worse for the truth."* Adenauer asked for the transfer of the case to Bonn.[2] In an interview with *Die Zeit* Globke again denied everything.[3]

In the meantime the BND under Reinhard Gehlen became active. Though internal supervision was the task of the BVS (Bundesverfassungsschutz) and the BND's task was external espionage Gehlen did not hesitate to keep Merten under surveillance. He suspected Merten to be in contact with the Communists and informed the CIA accordingly. The two organizations did not hesitate to cooperate in the supervision of Merten, Heinemann and the GVP.[4]

On 29 May 1961 the Bonn court gave notice that the case against Globke had been closed and preliminary proceedings against Merten had been open-

---

1 Bevers, *op. cit*, p. 169.

2 *"Die kommunistische Diffamierungskampagne gegen führende Persönlichkeiten in der Bundesrepublik, die sich zur Zeit vor allem auf Herrn Staatssekretär Dr. Globke konzentriert, ist zu meinem großen Bedauern durch die jüngsten Vorgänge in Frankfurt/M in ein neues Stadium getreten. Erstmalig ist es Vertretern des Ulbricht-Regimes gelungen, ihre zu den bekannten Angriffen gegen Staatssekretär Dr. Globke benutzten Materialien offiziell einem hohen Staatsorgan in der Bunderepublik, Herrn Generalstaatsanwalt Bauer, zu übergeben, Zeitungsnachrichten zufolge haben sie anschließend ihre Befriedigung darüber ausgesprochen, dass gerade Herr Generalstaatsanwalt Bauer, an dessen Objektivität ich persönlich natürlich in keiner Weise zweifle, ins Zwielicht gezogen, sondern auch das bei ihm anhängig gemachte Verfahren (...) politisch zu werden. Nichts könnte der Wahrheitsfindung weniger dienlich sein als dies." Ibidem*, p. 178f.

3 "Globke und die Juden" *Die Zeit* 8 (17. Februar 1961).

4 Archer, *op. cit.*, p. 52f,

ed. Merten complained against this at the superior court in Cologne. However, on 10 July 1962 the Cologne court rejected Merten's objection as unfounded.[1]

The trial began as late as October 1965. Quite a number of witnesses were heard. None of them had precise knowledge about the meeting of Merten with Eichmann. But some well known witnesses assured that Merten had committed himself for the Jews. He had warned them secretly, had organized passports for their evacuation and had bought free forced labour commandos. Robert Servatius, the defence lawyer of Eichmann, told the court that during the trial in Jerusalem he had asked Eichmann about Globke. The latter replied: *"Is this of any use for me? If not then let us leave Globke out of the game. Perhaps he is grateful to me."* In the Bonn trial Servatius expressed the opinion that Eichmann had met Merten and proved it by quotes from Eichmann. Politicians in Bonn hinted that the German delivery of weapons to Israel were the price that Globke was neither charged nor called as witness to the trial in Jerusalem When Globke's name was mentioned in the Jerusalem trial members of the German observer delegation immediately called Bonn. Eichman commented this behaviour of the "Globke-Garde:" *"Here we see his bad conscience."* Indeed, Globke was the only witness in the Bonn case who delivered his statements without having sworn an oath. Merten himself stated that he had been put under heaviest pressure by agents of the BND (Bundesnachrichtendienst) not to mention any relation between Eichmann and Globke. On the seventh day of the Bonn trial Merten did not appear because he had fallen sick[2]. Therefore the trial was adjourned for an indefinite time.[3] The trial was dismissed in 1968 three years before Merten's death in September 1971.

There is no other reliable proof for Merten's statement that Globke torpedoed the rescue of the 10,000 Jewish women and children. Eichmann denied it in his trial in Jerusalem and stated that he never met Merten,[4] which of course was a lie. On the other side Globke's assertion that he had been close to the 20th July resistance movement is scarcely credible. On the other side Merten's statements were certainly an act of revenge because Bonn had done almost nothing to free him from the Greek prison.

---

1 AA Poli. Archiv, Ref. 206, Bd. 135, 2 Ws 180/53/8 Js 323/6 + 8 Js/232/61.

2 *"Nutzt mir das etwas? Wenn nicht, dann wollen wir ihn (Globke) da herauslassen. Vielleicht ist er mir dankbar."* - *"Da sieht man das schlechte Gewissen."* P. St. "Juden-Deportation unter der Lupe eines Gerichts" *Die Zeit* 45 (1965) quoted from *Zeit Online*, "Max Merten contra Hans Globke" (22 November 2012).

3 "Merten-Prozeß vertagt" *Frankfurter Rundschau* (24. Oktober 1965).

4 Bevers, *op. cit.*, p. 192.

After his return to Germany Merten brought suit against Marbach who was now the president of the State Court of Accounts of Schleswig-Holstein, which was followed by the *Hamburger Echo*. On 16 September the trial of Marbach began. The prosecutory accused Marbach to have committed perjury when he made his statements during Merten's trial in Athens.[1] However, nothing happened. Indeed, on 28 January 1974 Marbach received one of the highest German decorations, the *Große Bundesverdienstkeuz mit Stern*.[2]

Another interesting aspect is the fact that Globke was assisted by the CIA since 1960. Together the German Secret Service (BND) and the CIA checked Merten's letters and listened to his telephone calls.[3]

Merten vs. Karamanlis and Makris

Merten's report about K. Karamanlis and D. Makris as well as the latter's wife Doxoula Leontidou is of a similar character . On 17 September 1960 the *Hamburger Echo* published the following story which was certainly inspired by Merten: On 23 November 1942 Doxoula allegedly said to Merten that two days later the Gorgopotamos railway bridge would be blown up. Allegedly Merten informed General Krenzki who did not take the story seriously, but sent some soldiers to the bridge. Most probably Merten invented this story, because from whom could the young woman have learned about the secret operation *Harling* the blowing up of the bridge by an SOE commando operation in cooperation with ELAS and EDES? Moreover the bridge was in the Italian zone of occupation. Then followed a passage even less credible: Merten allegedly knew *"that Doxoula's uncle, Konstantin, did not only make politics but also dabbled in the spy business. And this in a double function: As a member of the resistance movement and as a man of confidence of the German SD (Sicherheitsdienst). As the same was true for Doxoula's fiancé, Makris, Merten could not resist the begging of the Greek lady and allowed her to use the telephone line to Athens for talks with him. But, Merten remembered, their conversations were not only sweet nothings which made the wires tremble. To be an agent of the Germans paid. There was an order that Greek agents were rewarded by the confiscated properties of the Jews."*[4]

---

1 *Hamburger Echo* (16. September 1960).

2 Schleswig-Holsteinisches Landesarchiv Abt. 605, Nr. 3470.

3 Archer, *op. cot.*, p. 44

4 *"dass Doxoulas Onkel, Konstantin, in Athen nicht nur in Politik, sondern nebenher auch 'in Nachrichten machte'. Und zwar in doppelter Funktion: Einmal als Angehöriger der Widerstandsbewegung, dann als 'Vertrauensmann' des deutschen Sicherheitsdienstes. Da das gleiche auch für Doxoulas Verlobten, Makris, galt, hatte Merten der Bitte der Griechin nicht widerstehen können, die Fernmeldeleitung nach Athen zu Gesprächen mit ihm*

On 19 September the *Hamburger Echo* alleged further that Doxoula, her fiancé Makris and a lawyer from Serres, named Karamanlis, whose law office did not run well, obtained on trust the silk store of a Jew worth 15,000 pounds sterling as reward for their cooperation with the SD. Allegedly they had sold the store a little later making a huge profit. During the trial in Athens Doxoula said under oath that she had scarcely known Merten.[1] On 28 September *Der Spiegel* reported the affair also.[2]

This story also was also an invention by Merten, fact however is that Doxoula worked in Merten's office and was engaged to Makris and later married him. The statement that Karamanlis had worked for the resistance is absurd because the resistance (EAM/ELAS) was oriented to the left. Similarly absurd is the assertion that Karamanlis had worked for the SD. Karamanlis had always been a patriot and the allegation that he had enriched himself with Jewish stolen goods is malicious slander. It does not mesh with his character. Karamanlis never enriched himself during his whole career as a politician. The word uncle (θείος) does not necessarily describe a kinship relation it was used to describe a close friend of a family the German pet name is "Nennonkel".[3]

The articles in the *Hamburger Echo* and in *Der Spiegel* caused a great excitement in Athens. Deputies asked the government what they intended to do against the defamation. The AA in Bonn declared in its *Bulletin* without prior contacting the two press organs that the articles contained untrue claims and gross insults of the Greek Prime Minister. However the AA did not mention the content of the articles. The Greek Government threatened to file a complaint against the *Hamburger Echo*. Merten, however, repeated his accusations against Doxoula in a letter to the *Hamburger Echo* which was published: Doxoula had worked in Merten's office 18 months and then until March 1944 as his personal interpreter. In the trial in Athens, however, she had said under oath that she had briefly seen him only twice.[4]

---

benutzen zu dürfen. 'Doch', erinnert sich Merten, 'es war nicht nur Liebesgeflüster, was damals die Drähte zittern ließ.' In Griechenland Agent der Deutschen zu sein, zahlte sich aus: Es bestand eine fest verbindliche Anordnung, die griechischen Agenten durch das liquidierte jüdische Vermögen 'entsprechend' zu entschädigen." Claus Menzel, "Wenn Eichmann auspackt" *Hamburger Echo* (17. September 1960), p. 10.

1 *Ibidem* (19. September 1960), p. 10.

2 "Kriegsverbrechen Griechenland. Ihr Onkel Konstantin" *Der Spiegel* 40 (28. September 1960), p. 34.

3 Hans Henrich, "Dreyfus in der Bunderepublik" *Hamburger Echo* (29. September 1960), p. 2.

4 Claus Menzel, "Die griechische Regierung droht mit Strafantrag gegen das 'Hamburger

On 30 September the *Hamburger Echo* reported on its front page that the series of articles had triggered a governmental crisis in Athens and a gagging order had been issued for the Greek press: On 19 September the Athens prosecutor had warned all newspapers appearing in the capital to not reprint the articles of *the Echo* and the *Spiegel*. If they did the police would confiscate the papers. When on 21 September the conservative paper *Estia* dared to do it the Prime Minister had no other choice than to distance himself from the prosecution's act. The EDA asked the Government to dispel the doubts.[1] On 3 October it was learned that minister Makris had taken *Hamburger Echo, Der Spiegel* and Merten to court in Athens.[2]

On 12 October *Der Spiegel* published a press statement of the Greek Ambassador Ypsilantis which spoke of *"outrageous and slanderous"* accusations in the articles which *"served malicious purposes are cocoons of a morbid brain."* He denied statements which had not been mentioned in the articles but he did not utter one word concerning the real accusations and the facts mentioned in the articles. *Der Spiegel* listed them again and claimed in regard to Doxoula's statement under oath in Athens, that the Greeks suffered from a weak capacity for remembering. As a proof of their closer acquaintance *Der Spiegel* published the page from a photo album, which she had given to Merten as a present on Christmas 1942, with her handwritten dedication. *Der Spiegel* further proved that the official dementi of the Athens Government consisted out of the dementis of the AA and of Ypsilantis.[3]

The *Spiegel* author amused himself about the fact that Makris had filed his accusation against the German press organ in Athens though he knew that no court in Athens could do anything there against the German press. Merten on the other side had filed his accusation against Doxoula via the Greek General Consulate to the responsible law enforcement agency in Greece. In Athens Georgios Papandreou, a politician of the opposition, commented on this as: *"In case Merten proves his relations to Mrs. Makris no further trials must take place. Because the cabinet Karamanlis must resign."*[4]

Echo'" *Hamburger Echo* (29. September 1960), pp. 1 und 2.

1 *Ibidem* (30. September 1960), p. 1.

2 *Ibidem* (3. Oktober 1960).

3 *"ungeheuerlichen und verleumderischen" - "hinterhältigen Zwecken dienten, Gespinste eines krankhaften Hirns sind."* "Presse. Griechenland. Dementeritis praecox" *Der Spiegel* 42 (12. Oktober 1960), pp. 39-41. Merten said that in the album was a photo, which showed him and the other three protagonists. This photo was never published.

4 *"Falls Merten seine Beziehungen zu Frau Makris nachweise, brauchten keine weiteren Prozesse mehr geführt werden. Dann müsse das Kabinett Karamanlis abtreten." Ibidem*, p. 41; Spyros Linardatos, *Apo ton emfylio sti chounta*, IV, (Athens: Papazisis, 1986), p.

It is known that neither minister Makris nor the cabinet resigned. However on 10 November 1961 the Athenian district court condemned Merten to four years and the editorial journalists of *Hamburger Echo* and *Spiegel* to two years prison in absentia. Makris was to receive 70,000 Drachmae (about 9,300 DM) compensation. Makris had brought 35 witnesses to the court of which many could only say that they did not know anything of the collaboration of Makris or his present wife.[1] A different outcome could not be expected. Makris knew why he went to court in Greece and not in the Federal Republic.

After his return Merten to Germany Merten had submitted to the district office of Berlin Schöneberg an application of compensation for his "Greek passiontide" which was decided positively in summer 1961. Prisoners of war who returned after many years after the end of the war from the Soviet Union received such payments. On 4 August 1961 Merten received a first instalment of 300 DM per month.[2] In 1962 he submitted another application that in case of his death his wife and his son should receive a surviving dependants' pension. The Berlin administrative tribunal rejected this at first but then an extrajudicial compromise was found.[3] Max Merten died on 21 September 1971 at the age of 60.

---

561. There one finds critical comments by Pasalidis, Venizelos, Tsirimokos und Markezinis.

1 "Rückspiegel" *Der Spiegel* 32 (22. November 1961).

2 "Rückspiegel" *Der Spiegel* 32 (2. August 1961).

3 *Tagesspiegel* (23 Februar 1973).

"MERTEN'S TREASURES"

An Indiana Jones Story

Because Merten was involved in the handling of the confiscated Jewish properties the Greek side insinuated that he had enriched himself and had collected treasures. Allegedly he brought a small part to his wife who lived in Hungary at that time, a greater part he hid somewhere in Greece. This rumour circulated in Greece for decades as I personally remember it but nobody took it seriously.

But in 1999 the rumour assumed a new quality when a certain Konstantinos Vrettos contacted the Jewish community in Thessaloniki via his lawyer. He claimed that he knew where the treasures were that Merten had stolen from the Jews. Allegedly he had been a cell mate of Merten in the Averof jail. However, Merten had been in solitary confinement all the time. Merten had allegedly told him that his treasure consisted out of 46 crates with 230,000 golden pounds (sovereigns), one box with 300 huge diamonds and a Holy Chalice (!). 1944 he had taken his treasure by a submarine of the German navy to the Mycenaean gulf. Near Kalamata it was loaded on a kaiki with the help of three German officers and sunk at a certain bay into the sea. Then he allegedly shot the three officers to keep his secret and returned to Thessaloniki with the submarine. Vrettos enriched the story by mentioning people who had never existed. Vrettos declared himself ready to tell the Jewish community the place where the treasure was - contingent upon a payment of 200,000 Euros. It is unknown whether this sum was paid. Fact is, however, that in summer of 2,000 civil servants, private people and members of the Jewish community dived for the treasures. Greek TV was transmitting live. Of course nothing was found. In 2002 it became known that Vrettos was a criminal who had been in jail several times.[1]

Until now this tale could be considered as a grotesque story à la Indiana Jones over which one could be amused. How could Merten collect such a fortune from the Jewish community which in 1942 had not been able to raise the necessary sum of money and had been obliged to sell the cemetery to the town of Salonika. Why a Holy Chalice should have been among the jewelry of the Jews seems inexplicable. How Merten, a civil war administrator in the rank of a captain, could give orders to the captain of a submarine of the Navy (Kriegsmarine) is quite inexplicable too and this the more so because in summer 1944 not one German submarine was deployed in the Mediterranean.

---

1 *Βημαγαζίνο* (12. September 2004), pp. 68-73.

The idea that he had ordered it to come from Kiel is even more crazy since the boat could not have passed the narrows of Gibraltar.

Where did these three officers come from? Did they belong to the army or to the navy? Who sailed the kaiki? How did Merten explain to the submarine commander that the three officers had disappeared? Who sailed the kaiki back to the submarine and the submarine back to Salonika? The whole story is crazy and this the more so because Merten had left Salonika in March 1944, and was somewhere in the North, probably in Zagreb. As it israther improbable that Merten had the ability of bilocation the whole story was total nonsense.

But on 12 August 2000 MDR (Mitteldeutscher Rundfunk) reported in the news series *Brisant* about the diving action. In the sea in front of Kalamata a gold treasure was searched, *"Consisting out of gold bars, golden coins and jewels in today's value between 40 and 45 billion DM (!), which were sunk here in 1944. The treasures were taken from the Jews during during the occupation with the promise that they would not be deported. Initiator of this affair had been the German officer Dr. Max Merten and he had given the information about this to a close confidant. Alos the ZDF [second German TV]took over this story on 18 August in its 'Heute Journal'."*[1] In a letter to Wolfgang Breyer from the MDR one reads: *"Gold, jewels and religious objects, worth three to four billion Mark by guess - since Friday divers are searching o front of Greece's southwestern coast for these sunk Nazi treasures. NS-commander Max Merten took away these treasures from the Jews of the norther Greek harbour town of Thessaloniki promising that they would be spared deportation of 50,000 people to the extermination camps. But he loaded the treasures of a freighter and sunk it wantonly.[...] If the treasure of the Jews of Thessaloniki really existed will be proved when the search is successful. At the moment ten days diving are planned."*[2] It is difficult to state

---

1 *"bestehend aus Goldbarren, Goldmünzen und Juwelen im heutigen Wert von 40 bis 45 Mrd. DM (!), der hier 1944 versenkt worden sein soll. Diese Schätze sollen während der deutschen Besatzungszeit den Juden von Thessaloniki abgenommen worden sein mit dem Versprechen, dass sie dafür nicht deportiert werden würden. Initiator dieser Sache sei der deutsche Offizier Dr. Max Merten gewesen, und er habe die betreffende Information einem nahen Vertrauten gegeben. Auch das ZDF übernahm diesen Beitrag am 18. August in seinem 'Heute-Journal'."* Breyer, *op. cit.*, p. 81.

2 *"Gold, Juwelen und religiöse Gegenstände, schätzungsweise drei bis vier Milliarden Mark wert - seit Freitag suchen Taucher vor der Südwestküste Griechenlands nach diesem versunkenen Nazi-Schatz. NS-Kommandant Max Merten soll die Kostbarkeiten einst Juden in der nordgriechischen Hafenstadt Thessaloniki mit dem falschen Versprechen abgenommen haben, damit die Deportation von rund 50.000 Menschen in Vernichtungslager zu verhindern. Stattdessen soll er die gestohlenen Güter jedoch in einen Frachter geladen und denselben mutwillig versenkt haben. {...] Ob es den "Schatz der Juden von Thessa-*

what is more astonishing, the incompetence of the responsible editorial journalists or their total ignorance of Greek affairs.

---

loniki" wirklich gegeben hat, wird sich erst bei einer erfolgreichen Suche herausstellen. Zunächst sind zehn Tage für die Tauchgänge eingeplant." Letter of MDR to Breyer on 15 November 2000. Facsimile Breyer, *op.cit.*, p. 142.

CONCLUSIONS

The Merten case has nothing to do with justice. Here no criminal activities were expiated, Merten was not a war criminal. The Merten case was a political one. Of the German war criminals which had terrorized the Greeks not one was punished by the German judiciary. In Greece as well only a few members of military were convicted (Andrae) and another few were executed (Müller, Bräuer) but only right after the end of the war. There was no interest in numerous trials which would cost a lot, and would block the normal work of the judiciary for a long time. The condemnation of the war criminals was left to the Federal Republic. But from the very beginning Greece expected a financial trade-off for the suspension of the trials, beginning with the purchase of wine and tobacco, Greece's main export products.

However with the signing of the London Debt Agreement of 1953 the prospect for reparations sank. When in 1957 the Yugoslavs received camouflaged reparations of 300 million DM Greece demanded the same amount. When Germany delayed the negotiations the persecution of the war criminals was reactivated. The only one who fell into the trap was Max Merten. He became a kind of hostage to press through the Greek demands. When Bonn declared its readiness to pay 200 million DM disguised as an investment credit Karamanlis promised to set Merten free immediately after the end of the trial.

The trial was dealt with by a military court. As a civilian court the judges would have been obliged to check the truth of the statements of the witnesses of the prosecution. This would certainly have led to a much milder judgement if not even an acquittal. By the unchecked statements of the witnesses of the prosecution Merten could be stylised as a war criminal par excellence. The statements of the defence witnesses could be neglected. Thus Merten was sentenced to 25 years of prison. The case attracted a lot of political interest and thus Merten's release right after the end of the trial was impeded.

This was favourable for the Greek Government because in the meantime the negotiation of the general agreement of the compensation of the Jews moved forward and Merten's release could be used as a means of pressure in these negotiations. When the negotiations were on the way to the home stretch Merten was released. Thus Merten was used as a bargaining chip in both negotiations. Spiliotis is fully right when she writes: Merten *"Merten was the bargaining chip of the Greeks for their option on reparations."*[1]

1 *"war das Faustpfand der Griechen für ihre Option auf Entschädigungszahlungen."* Spiliotis, *op. cit.*, p. 155.

The analysis of the accusations against Merten shown in this study attested, that he was no war criminal and no anti-Semite. Of course one can accuse him that he did not oppose signing the orders which Wisliceny brought with him. However only a few would have dared to reject this because the consequences would certainly have been ackward if not even dangerous. Resistance could have meant martyrdom and who was ready for this. The only thing which one can accuse Merten of is that did not take this risk. Thus a certain amount of moral guilt can be stated at most. This, however, can be said about most Germans at that time. Merten as an administrative officer was in a difficult position but he did his job honestly. Generally speaking it can be stated that Merten did his work as administrative officer correctly.

Merten's double revenge actions after his release can be understood, however, the way he substantiated his accusations with dubious accusations show that he was a refined lawyer who attacked his opponent with all kinds of tricks. By his attack on Globke and the Greek trio he entered a terrain which would have been better to avoid. He behaved ineptly and naively and resorted to the same level as the others.

Spiliotis formulated the behaviour of Greece and the Federal Republic excellently when she wrote: *"The action maxims of the German and Greek policy makers excelled not only by a lack of sense of justice but disclosed a measure of moral unpretentiousness which made pure scorn out of the self-image of the Federal Republic but of Greece also as 'firm standing democracies'. With the political solution of the question of the war criminals the rapprochement of the two countries was enforced but the price was the suspension of justice."*[1] One can only agree with this statement. Indeed in this case injustice was done in order to achieve the aim, by making an "innocent" into a "war criminal" simply because there was no real German war criminal.

The accusation that Merten had been an evil war criminal has remained in the Greek public to this day. During the recent financial crisis it was revived in order to prove that the Germans are still Nazis and were aiming at the erection of a fourth Reich. And it opened the door to a renewed demand of

---

1 *"Die Handlungsmaximen der deutschen und griechischen Entscheidungsträger zeichneten sich nicht nur durch einen Mangel an 'Rechtsgefühl' aus; vielmehr offenbarte sich ein Maß an moralischer Anspruchslosigkeit, das dem Selbstverständnis der Bundesrepublik, aber auch Griechenlands als 'firm standing democracies' Hohn sprach. Mit der politischen Lösung der Kriegsverbrecherfrage wurde vielleicht die Widerannäherung beider Länder nach dem Krieg forciert; doch der Preis dafür war die 'Suspendierung der Gerechtigkeit'." Ibidem*, p. 158.

payment of reparations. To this was added the demand of the repayment of the so-called enforced occupation loan which had never existed.[3]

The Merten affair had led to a great public emotional uproar and revived anti-German resentments which have continued to exist to the present. Whenever the government considers it necessary, they can be revived and used to try to obtain financial help in order to close a gap in the budget.

Concluding remarks

In this study we have seen that neither the military court nor the press believed that any German officer would have been prepared to help the Jews, and in many Greek circles this is still so. Many Greeks believe that the Germans were and are Nazis and are heading to establish the fourth Reich. True, Merten was a member of the Nazi party but he was never an ideologically convinced Nazi. He had preserved a sense of humanity which explains why he tried to help the Jews. Merten was not politically minded during the war. To a certain degree he was even naive. He developed a sense for politics only when he entered the Heinemann GVP party after the foundation of the FRG in 1949 which can be considered that he was a democrat then.

However, the Merten case was not unique. There were more who helped the Jews. One of the most prominent cases is that of Georg Eckert, who did the same, e.g he transported Jews with lorries into the mountains where they could disappear. His motives were political. Having been a leading member of SPD in the Weimar Republic he was against the regime and did his best to help not only the Jews but the Greeks also. He was chief of the meteorological station of the navy in Thessaloniki and head of a resistance organisation of German Social Democrats. He was in close contact with EAM/ELAS and saved Thessaloniki from being destroyed and, when the German army withdrew, he and his group joined ELAS. His liaison officer of ELAS was Georgios Dimitrakos the later Greek director of the German school in Athens. Eckert and his resistance group was highly praised by the people of Salonika for what they had done. When the German army withdrew, he and his group remained in the town. EAM members saw in his work the beginning of a new relation between Greece and Germany. I wrote a detailed account on Eckert's and Dimitrakos' activities and am preparing a new account in English.[4]

---

3 Heinz A. Richter, *Mythen und Legenden in der griechischen Zeitgeschichte* (Ruhpolding: Rutzen, 2016), pp. 103-113.

4 Heinz A. Richter, "Sozialdemokratischer Widerstand im besetzten Griechenland: Georg Eckert und seine Gruppe" *THETIS* 7 (2000), pp. 237-252 and Idem, "Georgios Dimitrakos:

And there is another prominent personality who helped Greece. This was General Felmy, the commander of the Army in southern Greece and Attika: In summer 1944 he received the order by Hitler to destroy Athens and blow up the Marathon dam before the German Army retreated. He knew that general Choltitz had been sentenced to death in absentia when he disobeyed a parallel order to destroy Paris but Felmy who was a simple honest soldier did not want to obey to this brutal order and managed to quit Athens without one shot fired with the help of two archaeologists.[1] It is not only unhistorical but sad that nowadays Felmy is considered a Nazi in certain circles in Athens.

From my own experience I know that any criticism of the behaviour of the Greeks in the past can lead to the accusation of making Nazi propaganda. But I am not alone in this. The British historian Antony Beevor was denounced as a Nazi by the Russians because he objectively described the crimes of the Red Army. Self-criticism is apparently not a habit of some peoples. Unfortunately those Germans who cared for Greece are no longer remembered there.

Petros Markaris explained this behaviour to the point: The Greeks pull their country to pieces when they are among themselves. If, however, a foreigner dares to utter any criticism they defend their country with tooth and claw.[2] One can only hope that this study contributes a bit to a change.

Widerstandskämpfer Humanist, Europäer" *THETIS* 7 (2000), pp. 253-284.

1 Heinz A. Richter, "General Hellmuth Felmy und die Rettung Athens" in: Heinz A. Richter (ed.), *Aspekte neugriechischer Geschichte. Gesammelte Aufsätze* (Wiesbaden: Harrassowitz, 2018)

2 Petros Markaris, *Zahltag. Ein Fall für Kostas Charitos* (Zürich; Diogens, 2012), p. 246.

BIBLIOGRAPHY

Primary Sources:

Files and Dokumentations

Germany

Zentrale Stelle Ludwigsburg (ZstL) 508 AR-Z139/59, Einstellungsverfügung der Staatsanwaltschaft Berlin vom 4.Juni 1968, Prozessgeschichte,

Auswärtiges Amt Referat 206 Band Nr. 134

Archiv für Christlich Demokratische Politik I-070-082/2

AG Tiergarten 353 AR 1680/61

Schleswig-Holsteinisches Landesarchiv,Abt. 605, Nr. 3470

United States

United States, Department of State, *Foreign Relations of the United States 1945,* VIII (Washington: Government Printing Office, 1969)

- *Foreign Relations of the United States 1955-1957,* XXIV (Washington: Government Printing Office, 1990)

Secondary Sources

Memoirs, Diaries, Remembrances

Neubacher, Hermann *Sonderauftrag Südost 1940-1945. Bericht eines fliegenden Diplomaten* (Seeheim: Buchkreis, 1966)

Merci, Lucilo : http://www.gemeinde.bozen.it/UploadDocs/6755_Merci_-deutsch.pdf

Secondary literature

A

Aly, Götz *Europa gegen die Juden 1880-1945* (Frankfurt: S. Fischer, 2017)

Apostolopoulos, Dimitrios *Die griechisch-deutschen Nachkriegsbeziehungen* (Frankfurt: Peter Lang, 2004)

Apostolou, Andrew "'The Exception of Salonika': Bystanders and Collaborators in Northern Greece" *Holocaust and Genocide Studies* 14:2 (2000), pp. 165-196

Archer, William D. "The Merten Affair." MA Thesis (Sacramento: State University, 2016

B

Benbassa, Esther *Die Geschichte der Sephardischen Juden. Von Toledo bis Saloniki* (Bochum: Winkler, 2005)

Bevers, Jürgen *Der Mann hinter Adenauer. Hans Globkes Aufstieg vom NS-Juristen zur Grauen Eminenz der Bonner Republik* (Berlin: Christoph Links, 2009)

Bowman, Steven "Another Righteous Gentile: The IRRC Representative in Salonika" *Thetis* 3 (1996)

Breyer, Wolfgang "Dr. Max Merten - ein Militärbeamter der deutschen Wehrmacht im Spannungsfeld zwischenLegenden und Wahrheit" Diss. (Mannheim, 2002)

Buchheim, Christoph "Das Londoner Schuldenabkommen", in: Ludolf Herbst (ed.): *Westdeutschland 1945–1955. Unterwerfung, Kontrolle, Integration* (München; Oldenbourg, 1986)

C-E

Dimitrakos, Giorgios *Απολογισμός και απολογία "από του φοβερού βήματος..."* (Athen: Polytypo, 1991)

Dordanas, Stratos and Vaios Kalogrias, "Die jüdische Gemeinde von Thessaloniki während der deutschen Besatzungszeit 1941-1944: Zwischengemeindliche Beziehungen, Ghettoisierung und Deportation" *PaRDeS Zeitschrift der Vereinigung für Jüdische Studien* 17 (Potsdam, 2011)

F

Favez, Jean-Claude *Une mission impossible? Le CICR, les déportations et les camps de concentrations nazi* (Lausanne, 1988)

Fleischer, Hagen *Im Kreuzschatten der Mächte. Griechenland 1941-1944* (Frankfurt, Bern, New York: Peter Lang, 1986)

- "Saloniki unter dem Hakenkreuz" Vortrag (Thessaloniki, 15. März 2011)

- "Der Neubeginn in den Deutsch-Griechischen Beziehungen nach dem Zweiten Weltkrieg und die 'Bewältigung' der jüngsten Vergangenheit", in: Institute of Balkan Studies (ed.), *Griechenland und die Bundesrepublik Deutschland im Rahmen Nachkriegseuropas* (Thessaloniki: IMXA, 1989)

Fleischer, Hagen & Despina Konstantinakou, „Ad calendas graecas? Griechenland und die deutsche Wiedergutmachung", in: Hans Günter Hockerts,, Claudia Moisel & Tobias Winstel, /eds.) *Grenzen der Wiedergutmachung: die Entschädigung für NS-Verfolgte in West- und Osteuropa,* (Göttingen, 2006)

G

Gilbert, Harald *Der Krieg in der Ägäis 1943-1944* (Wiesbaden: Harrassowitz, 2018)

"Globke. Ein unbedeutender Mann" *Der Spiegel* 8 (15. Februar 1961)

"Globke und die Juden" *Die Zeit* 8 (17. Februar 1961)

Görtemaker, Manfred & Christoph Safferling, *Die Akte Rosenberg. Das Bundesministerium der Justiz und die NS-Zeit* (München: Beck, 2016)

"Griechenland: Ihr Onkel Konstantin" *Der Spiegel* 40 (28. September 1960)

"Griechenland Beziehungen. Die Falle der Fahndung" *Der Spiegel* 21 (22. Mai 1957),

H

Haguel, "History of the Jews of Thessaloniki and the Holocuast" ACADEMIA

Hassid, Samuel "The Trial of Max Merten in the Changing Mirros of Time and Place", in: http://greece.haifa.ac.il/events/holocaust_greece/Samuel_-Hassid.pdf

Henrich, Hans "Dreyfus in der Bunderepublik" *Hamburger Echo* (29. September 1960)

I-J

Institute of Balkan Studies (ed.), *Griechenland und die Bundesrepublik Deutschland im Rahmen Nachkriegseuropas* (Thessaloniki: IMXA, 1989)

K-L

Klein, Wolfgang "Der Merten Prozess", in: www.dwkberlin.de

Kralowa, Katerina *Das Vermächtnis der Besatzung. Deutsch-griechische Beziehungen seit 1940* (Köln: Böhlau, 2016)

"Kriegsverbrechen Griechenland. Ihr Onkel Konstantin" *Der Spiegel* 40 (28. September 1960)

Lazaridou, Olga *Von der Krise zur Normalität, Die deutsch-griechischen Beziehungen unter besonderer Berücksichtigung der politischen und wirtschaftlichen Grundlagen (1949-1958)* Diss. (Bonn, 1992)

Linardatos, Spyros *Apo ton emfylio sti chounta,* II (Athen: Papazisis, 1977)

M

Mätzing, Heike Christina *Georg Eckert 1912-1974. Von Anpassung, Widerstand und Völkerverständigung* (Bonn: Dietz, 2018)

McNeill, William Hardy *Greece: American Aid in Action 1947-1956* (New York: The Twentieth Century Fund, 1957)

Menzel, Claus "Wenn Eichmann auspackt" *Hamburger Echo* (17. September 1960)

- "Die griechische Regierung droht mit Strafantrag gegen das 'Hamburger Echo'"*Hamburger Echo* (29. September 1960),

"Merten-Prozeß vertagt" *Frankfurter Rundschau* (24. Oktober 1965).

Molho, Michael *On Memoriam. Hommage aux Vitimes Juives des Nazis en Grèce* (Salonique:1948)

Molho, Rena *Der Holocaust der griechischen Juden. Studien zur Geschichte und Erinnerung* (Bonn: Dietz, 2016)

Meyer, Hermann Frank *Von Wien nach Kalavryta. Die blutige Spur der 117. Jäger-Division durch Serbien und Griechenland* (Mannheim: Bibliopolis, 2002).

N-R

"Presse. Griechenland. Dementeritis praecox" *Der Spiegel* 42 (12. Oktober 1960)

"Reparationen. Dein Maul zu halten" *Der Spiegel* (22. Oktober 1952)

Richter, Heinz A. *Griechenland im Zweiten Weltkrieg August 1939 - Juni 1941* [2](Ruhpolding: Rutzen, 2011)

- *Mythen und Legenden in der griechischen Zeitgeschichte* (Ruhpolding:Rutzen, 2016)
- *Griechenland zwischen Revolution und Konterrevolution 1936 - 1946* (Frankfurt: Europäische Verlagsanstalt, 1973
- *Geschichte Griechenlands im 20. Jahrhundert,* II, *1939-2004* (Ruhpolding: Rutzen, 2015), pp. 194, 210.
- "Sozialdemokratischer Widerstand im besetzten Griechenland: Georg Eckert und seine Gruppe" *THETIS* 7 (2000), pp. 237-252
- "Georgios Dimitrakos: Widerstandskämpfer Humanist, Europäer" *THETIS* 7 (2000), pp. 253-284
- "General Hellmuth Felmy und die Rettung Athens" in: Heinz A. Richter (ed.), *Aspekte neugriechischer Geschichte. Gesammelte Aufsätze* (Wiesbaden: Harrassowitz, 2018)

Rumpf, Helmut "Die deutsche Frage und die Reparationen" *http://www.zaoerv.de* (1973).

S

Saltiel, Leon "Dehumanazing the Dead. The Destruction of Thessaloniki's Jewish Cemetery in the Light of New Sources" *Akademia Edu*

Schramm, Ehrengard *Ein Hilfswerk für Griechenland. Begegnungen und Erfahrungen mit Hinterbliebenen deutscher Gewalttaten der Jahre 1941-1944* (Göttingen: Vandenhoeck & Ruprecht, 2003),

Spiliotis, Susanne-Sophia “Der Fall Merten, Athen 1959: Ein Kriegsverbrecherprozeß im Spannungsfeld Von Wiedergutmachungs- und Wirtschaftspolitik” MA-Thesis (München,1991)

- “‘An Affair of Politics, Not Justice’ The Merten Trial (1957-1959) and Greek-German Relations”, in: Mark Mazower (ed.), *After the War Was Over. Reconstructing the Family, Nation and State in Greece, 1943-1960* (Princeton: UP, 2000)

St. P. “Juden-Deportation unter der Lupe eines Gerichts” *Die Zeit* 45 (1965) quoted from *Zeit Online*, “Max Merten contra Hans Globke” (22 November 2012)

Stergiou, Andreas *Im Spagat zwischen Solidarität und Realpolitik. Die Beziehungen zwischen der DDR und Griechenland und das Verhältnis der SED zur KKE* (Möhnesee: Bibliopolis, 2001)

Svolopoulos, Konstantinos (ed.), *Konstantinos Karamanlis. Archeio gegonota kai keimena,* Vol. III, *Oktaetia dimiourgias 1956-1963* (Athen: Idryma Konstantinos Karamanlis, 1994)

T-Z

Weber, Gerhard “Zu den Generalsprozessen. Unterschiede der Verfahren und Urteile über deutsche Besatzungsgeneräle in Griechenland” *Thetis* 18 (2011)

INDEX OF NAMES

Auf den folgenden Seiten folgt ein Verzeichnis
weiterer Peleusbände.

Band 58 **Thorsten Kruse,**
Bonn - Nikosia - Ostberlin. Innerdeutsche Fehden auf fremdem Boden 1960-1972 (2013) 17x24, 400 Seiten, 67 Fotos auf 32 Tafeln, hard cover, ISBN 978-3-447-06766-9 EAN: 9783447067669, € 49.-

Band 59 **Heinz A. Richter,**
Griechenland 1940-1950. Die Zeit der Bürgerkriege (2012) 17x24, ca. 550 Seiten, 20 Karten, 1 herausnehmbare Faltkarte, 150 Fotos auf 64 Tafeln, hard cover, € 49.-, ISBN 978-3-447-06704-1 EAN: 9783447067041,

Band 60 **Heinz A. Richter,**
Griechenland 1950-1974. Zwischen Demokratie und Diktatur (2013) 600 Seiten, 125 Fotos, Hardcover, gebunden, € 49, ISBN 978-3-447-08908-3

Band 61 **Mihailo Popovic,**
Historische Geographie und Digital Humanities. Eine Fallstudie zum spätbyzantinischen und osmanischen Makedonien (2013) ca. 300 Seiten, 33 Abbildungen, 44 Karten, 8°, hard cover, ISBN 978-3-447-06950-2 € 32.-

Band 62 **Joachim Franz, Rosmarie Günther und Reinhard Stupperich (Hrsg.)**
„Ein Wald von Statuen" Kolloquium zum 20jährigen Bestehen der Antikensaal-Galerie in Mannheim und zur Begründung der Kurpfälzer Abguss-Sammlung vor 300 Jahren 300 Seiten, zahlreiche Abbildungen, Hardcover, gebunden, ISBN 978-3-447-10302-2, € 37.-

Band 63 **Harald Gilbert,**
Das besetzte Kreta 1941-1945 (2015) 404 Seiten, 47 sw und 8 farbige Abbildungen, 1 Landkarte, Hardcover, gebunden, € 49, ISBN 978-3-447-10186-8

Band 64 **Harry Cliadakis** (ed. Heinz Richter)
Fascism in Greece (2014) 147 pages, 34 photos, hard cover, threadbound, € 39.- ISBN978-3-447-10188-2,

Band 65,1 **Heinz A. Richter**
Krieg im Südosten I, Gallipoli 1915 (2014) 340 Seiten, 120 Fotos, 17 Karten, 1 Faltkarte, gebunden, € 42, ISBN 978-3-447-10118-9

Band 65,2 *Krieg im Südosten II, Makedonien 1915-1918* (2014) 250 Seiten, 91 Fotos, 4 Karten, gebunden, € 35, ISBN 978-3-447-10249-0

Band 66 *Von Mainz nach Kreta im Winter 1942-43. Das Reisetagebuch des "Künstlersoldaten" Rudo Schwarz.* (2015) 150 Seiten, 91 Seiten mit Reproduktionen des Tagebuchs und von Skizzen, 51 Fotos, Hardcover, gebunden, ISBN 978-3-447-10304-6, € 32.- (ed. Heinz Richter)

Band 67,1 **Heinz A. Richter,**
Geschichte Griechenlands im 20. Jahrhundert, Band 1: 1900-1939, (2015) 350 Seiten, 4 Karten, Hardcover, gebunden, 40 Euro, ISBN 978-3-447-10396-5

Band 67,2 **Heinz A. Richter,**
Geschichte Griechenlands im 20. Jahrhundert, Band 2: 1939-2004, (2015) 467 Seiten, 9 Karten, Hardcover, gebunden, 49Euro, ISBN 978-3-447-10398-5

Band 68 **Heinz A. Richter**
Griechenland 1915-1917 im Spiegel russischer Akten (2016) 118 Seiten, Hardcover, 28 Euro, 2015 ISBN 978-3-447-10612-2

Band 69 **Heinz A. Richter**
Griechenland 1945-46. Die britische Intervention (2016) 456 Seiten, 39 Fotos, gebunden, 49 Euro, ISBN 978-3-447-10533-0

Band 70 **Heinz A. Richter** (ed.),
Griechenland 1942-43. Erinnerungen von Elisabeth und Konstantinos Logothetopoulos (2015) 320 Seiten, 3 Abbildungen, Hardcover, 28 Euro, ISBN 978-3-447-10460-9

Band 71 **Johannes Fouquet** und **Lydia Gaitanou,**
Im Schatten der Alten? Ideal und Lebenswirklichkeit im römischen Griechenland (2016) 193 Seiten, zahlreiche Karten und Fotos, gebunden, 40 Euro, ISBN 978-3-447-10450-0

Band 72 **Heinz A. Richter**
Der griechisch-türkische Krieg 1919-1922 (2016) 222 Seiten, 132 Fotos, 18 Karten, 1 Faltkarte, gebunden, 30 Euro, ISBN 978-3-447-10656-6

Band 73 **Heinz A. Richter**
The Greek-Turkish War 1919-1922 (2016) 211 pages, 132 photos, 18 maps, 1 folded map, hardcover, 30 Euro, ISBN 978-3-447-10671-9

Band 74 **Heinz A. Richter,**

Mythen und Legenden in der griechischen Zeitgeschichte (2016) 116 Seiten, geb. 19,80 Euro, ISBN 978-3-447-10703-7

Band 76 **Heinz A. Richter**,
Hellas und Zypern in meinem Leben. Erinnerungen eines Zeithistorikers (2017) 236 Seiten, geb. 56 Tafeln mit 128 Fotos, 30 Euro, 2017; ISBN 978-3-447-10769-3

Band 77 **Heinz A. Richter**,
Geschichte der griechischen Linken (2017) 560 Seiten, 99 Fotos, geb., 50 Euro, 2017; ISBN 978-3-447-10846-1

Band 78 **Harald Gilbert,**
Der Krieg in der Ägäis 1943-1944 (2018) 394 Seiten, 40 Tafeln mit 52 Abb., 16 farbige und 6 sw Karten, 1 farbige Faltkarte, geb., 40 Euro, ISBN 978-3-447-10913-0

Band 79 **Heinz A. Richter**,
Geschichte der zypriotischen Linken (2017) 248 Seiten, 16 Tafeln mit 47 Fotos, geb., 30 Euro, ISBN 978-3-447-10867-6

Band 80 **Heinz A. Richter**,
Die türkischen Meerengen in der internationalen Politik 1900-1917 (2018) 274 Seiten, 32 Tafeln mit 77 Fotos, 7 Karten, 1 herausnehmbare farbige Faltkarte, geb., 40 Euro, ISBN 978-3-447-10915-4

Band 84 **Heinz A. Richter**,
Das Osmanische Reich im Ersten Weltkrieg bis zum Friedensschluss 1924 (2018) 274 Seiten, 32 Tafeln mit 103 Fotos, 32 Karten, 1 herausnehmbare Faltkarte, geb., 40 Euro, ISBN 978-3-447-11038-9

Band 85 **Heinz A. Richter**,
The Ottoman Empire in WWI until the Peace in 1924 (2018) 256 pages, 32 plates with over 100 photos, 32 maps, 1 folded map, hard cover, 40 Euro, ISBN 978-3-447-11045-7

Band 86 **Heinz A. Richter**,
Die Griechen im Osmanischen Reich 1913-1923. Ihre Verfolgung und Vertreibung (2018),198 Seiten, 32 Tafeln mit über 60 Fotos, 6 Karten, 1 herausnehmbare Faltkarte, geb., 40 Euro, ISBN 978-3-447-11131-7

Band 87 **Heinz A. Richter**,
The Greeks in the Ottoman Empire 1913-1923. Their Persecution and Expulsion (2018) 188pages, 32 plates with over 60 photos, 6 maps, one folded map in the back, hard cover, 40 Euro, ISBN 978-3-447-11150-8

Band 88 **Heinz A. Richter** (ed.),
Aspekte neugriechischer Geschichte (2018) 132 Seiten, viele Fotos, geb., 30 Euro, ISBN 978-3-447-11132-4

Band 89 **Heinz A. Richter**,
Modern Greek Myths (2019), 104 pages, hard cover, 19,80 Euro, ISBN 978-3-447-11165-2

Band 90 **Heinz A. Richter**,
German-Greek Relation 1940-1960 and the Merten Affair (2019) 116 pages, 12 pages plates, hard cover, 20 Euro, ISBN 978-3-447-11177-5

Band 91 **Heinz A. Richter**,
Greece 1936-1946 Events and People (2019) 186 pages, 21 photos, 1 map, hard cover, 30 Euro, ISBN 978-3-447-11241-3

Bezugsquelle: Harrassowitz-Verlag, Kreuzberger Ring 7b-d, 65174 Wiesbaden
E-Mail: verlag@harrassowitz.de